HANNAH - So
great to meet you.
You are special!

# SHATTERED
## IMAGE

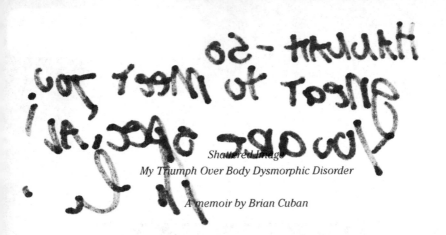

*Shattered Image*
*My Triumph Over Body Dysmorphic Disorder*

*A memoir by Brian Cuban*

Library of Congress Cataloging-in-Publication Data
Cuban, Brian
Shattered Image: My Triumph Over Body Dysmorphic Disorder
p. cm
ISBN 9780988879584 (paperback)

Printed in the United States of America

While all the individuals in this story are real, where appropriate,
names have been changed to protect their privacy.

# SHATTERED IMAGE

## My Triumph Over
## Body Dysmorphic Disorder

A memoir by
## Brian Cuban

Published by NetMinds

*To my father, who taught me the meaning of family.*
*Never let it go. Never abandon it.*
*To my brothers Mark and Jeff, who never abandoned me.*
*To my mom, who came back to me.*
*To Amanda, who understood me.*
*To Angelo, who was there for me.*

*I would also like to acknowledge the following people, without whose advice and inspiration* Shattered Image *would not have become a reality: Barbara Cuban (in memoriam), Gerald Melchiode, MD, Bob Beaudine, Scott Greenfield, Esq., Brian Tannebaum, Esq., Antonin (Nino) Pribetic, Esq., Maria Dorfner, Larry North, Jacquelyn Ekern, MS, LPC, and Andrea Barthwell, MD.*

❖

*How the pieces of* **Shattered Image**
*were put together...*

This book was produced via NetMinds, a team-publishing platform that enables authors to find and join forces with talented editors, designers, marketers, and other publishing professionals. We offer our authors the ability to grant each team member a stake in the book's long-term financial success, just like a startup. NetMinds' authors enjoy the luxury of autonomy combined with skilled expertise.

To start a project or join a team, visit NetMinds.com.

***Contributors***
**Author:** Brian Cuban
*briancuban.com*
**Structural Editor:** Luke Gerwe
**Cover Photography:** James Bland
*JamesBland.com*
**Book Design:** Robert Greeson
*RobertGreeson.com*
**Media Relations:** Rubenstein Public Relations
*rubensteinpr.com*
**Project Mentor:** Tim Sanders
*my.netminds.com/timsanders*

# Table of Contents

*The shy, happy child before the storm.*

# INTRODUCTION:
## *The Down and Dirty of BDD*

*I* have a number of recurring dreams: Scenes from law school, struggles with addiction, and failed relationships are all in rerun. These dreams are vivid and colorful, like full-length movies played out in my subconscious. They say this is common with recovering addicts.

One particular dream begins as I arrive at a party. I'm by myself as I walk into a dark, empty room with a bar and a bartender. I don't want to be alone, and I wait for familiar faces to appear. I know old high school classmates will be showing up, and I want to be included in their fun. I order a Diet Coke. The bartender tells me they don't serve non-alcoholic drinks. Instead, he offers me a Jack Daniels and Diet Coke, my drink of choice pre-sobriety. I take the drink from him, but I can't raise the glass to my mouth. My right arm is frozen.

I decide that, if I can't drink, I'll go do a line of cocaine instead. I push off from the bar and head to the bathroom. I line up the coke in front of me, but I can't snort it. The white line is just out of reach of the straw, and then the powder vaporizes into the ether of the dream. Now I have neither drugs nor alcohol to help me transform into that other, more confident Brian. The Brian I want to see in the mirror every morning. The Brian I hardly ever see.

I'm out of the bathroom and walking through the room. I see a high school classmate. He says he's my friend, but he doesn't like me. I can sense it. For some reason, he's still sixteen, though I'm now fifty-one. As I approach him, he makes a comment about how fat I still am. I'm mortified, and I head back to the bathroom. The image in the mirror is fine: I am no longer a heavy teenager. I am a grown, mature adult. *Why is he making fun of my weight? Doesn't he see me?*

The room is filling up. More high school classmates. They're all teens. How did I get so old? I ask if I can join the group. They all laugh or otherwise ignore me. *I'm right here! You know me!* The room gets darker. I can no longer see them. The familiar feeling, the familiar ache. Now I'm standing against the gym wall at the high school dance, wishing someone would talk to me. My childhood bullies appear again. They start pulling at my clothes, tearing them off, exposing me. I'm crying and screaming. *Why don't you like me!* They laugh in response.

Suddenly I'm awake. As I adjust to the light streaming in the window, the ache of the dream is still with me. Hopefully, a different rerun tomorrow night. I pull myself out of bed and prepare myself for the day.

The feeling of the dream fades, but morning brings decisions that will have consequences for both the mind and body. The choices I make through the daytime can leave me feeling calm and happy by sundown, or feeling like I'm still stuck in a nightmare. This is the reality I face every morning. This is the reality of body dysmorphic disorder.

•

This is the story of my struggle with, and recovery from, a compulsive behavior clinically known as body dysmorphic disorder (BDD). That struggle has included recovery from bulimia, anorexia, alcoholism, and addiction to cocaine and steroids. I also suffer from clinical depression. For decades, I engaged in self-destructive behavior with the single goal of correcting a terribly distorted sense of self-image.

BDD is a condition that often begins in adolescence and affects as many as one to two percent of the U.S. population, both male and female. For potentially millions of Americans, depression, addiction, eating disorders, and broken relationships are common by-products of the disorder. My goal with this book is to help other BDD sufferers identify and avoid destructive behaviors in their lives; replace them with positive, fulfilling behaviors; and encourage other readers to reach out to friends or family members who may be suffering from BDD. I'll also describe my battles with addiction, eating disorders, and those other destructive behaviors that are often by-products of the disorder (and that many non-BDD sufferers might relate to).

I hope that, by sharing my experiences, I can help

others know that they are not alone and encourage them to seek treatment.

Becoming obsessed with appearance and allowing that obsession to lead to self-destructive behavior did not happen to me overnight. I did not suddenly wake up one day and see a distorted image in the mirror, an image I hated and was afraid of. It was a life-long process of negative experiences building on each other, triggering innate psychological tendencies. One of the keys to recovery for me was getting honest about those formative experiences. A path to BDD recovery probably will not be successful if it is grounded in denial and lies.

An important disclaimer: If you suspect that you or someone you know suffers from BDD, it is important to talk to a professional. This book does not constitute professional medical advice, and the path I took to recovery may not be possible or appropriate for everyone. I hope, however, that this book helps open up a new conversation about BDD. Body dysmorphia is still not fully understood and is unfamiliar to many Americans. If this book helps people understand that groups of symptoms such as anorexia, low self-esteem, depression, addiction, muscle dysmorphia, and self-destructive behaviors can often be linked to a condition that is both diagnosable and treatable, then I have done my job.

•

So what is the down and dirty of BDD? Experts generally characterize it as a condition marked by a sometimes-disabling preoccupation with imagined or exaggerated defects of physical appearance. As has been the case for me, many symptoms of BDD are similar to those of obsessive-compulsive disorder (OCD), involving daily compulsive routines designed to relieve shameful and stressful feelings of a distorted body image. BDD affects millions of Americans and countless others around the world. It has been known to psychiatrists for more than a century. Still, BDD isn't widely discussed in the American media. In recent decades, body dysmorphia may have taken a back seat in clinical diagnoses to eating disorders, partly because BDD and eating disorders can overlap or be closely related, and eating disorders have simply had more high-profile media attention in this country. But attention for BDD is growing, thanks to the work of researchers such as Dr. Katharine A. Phillips and others.

But how do people develop body dysmorphic disorder? Psychologists, psychiatrists, and other treatment professionals will tell you that there is no one cause for BDD. Recent studies hint that BDD may be a unique form of psychological hardwiring that some are simply born with, but our early-life experiences are closely tied to the symptoms we develop as we age.

How did it develop for me? Mental health professionals would argue (and you may know from personal experience) that the sort of BDD-forming experiences I encountered in adolescence—bullying, family strife, and social isolation—are not unique. Life happens to us all. However, we all respond differently. Biological factors such as genetic predisposition, the psychological influences in your life, and environment all can play a role in the emergence of BDD. Is there an exact point in life that I can point to and say, "This is when my thought process changed, this is when I developed BDD?" No, there isn't. Maybe, if I had a time machine, I could go back to that ten- or eleven-year-old, bullied, shy, and self-conscious child and say, "a-ha!" As it stands, many decades later, memories blend together. Memories can be faulty. What I can say I am sure of is this: It was like building the foundation of a house. Negative experiences, including bullying, without a safe place to talk about them and without treatment outlets, were the bricks. My innately obsessive-compulsive thought process was the mortar keeping those experiences in place.

But aside from the cause and effect, what does BDD actually feel like? Here are some of the behaviors that have defined my struggle over the years. To a casual observer, some of these may seem narcissistic, quirky, or eccentric. I call them my "BDD tics." They have come and gone over the course of my life, and they may sound familiar to others with BDD. Maybe you are engaging in one or more of these behaviors but don't know if you have BDD or not. Maybe you or someone you know has a set of unique tics. These quirky behaviors can be harmless in themselves, but they may be the sign of a deeper problem.

1. ***The shower inspection.*** When my BDD self-doubt was at its worst, I'd never fail to spend long stretches in the shower engaged in detailed inspection of the areas of "concern" on my body. I knew I was doing it, I knew it was strange, but it had become integrated into my daily routine. With the palm of my hand, I would press down on my stomach and try to flatten it. Of course, it always bounced back, but I felt like I could actually detect any increase in my waist size. There was also the "trunk twist" to each side where I would look for increased fat on each of my love handles. Then I'd run my right hand down the left side of my rib cage starting just under the armpit. I truly believed I could feel even a minute increase of fat in proportion to my ribs and back. In my mind, I could see the extra curvature if I had lost weight or the "filling in" if I had gained weight. My fingers would press into my skin, acting like a tire gauge. Has the stick gone up or down? My outlook for the day would change for the better or worse with each inspection. These days, my time in the shower is more about lather-rinse-repeat and less about repetitive self-scrutiny.

2. ***Verifying perceived body defects through touch.*** This is different from the shower routine. It is done often unconsciously in public, and, as with the shower inspection, I still do it from time to time. I could be walking down the street, in a mall, or sitting at dinner. For a split second, I will touch my chest. It is not unusual for me to sit with my right hand over the left side of my chest. Checking. Reassuring myself that it feels right. I often won't even know that I'm doing it, but those around me will. A friend once asked me jokingly if I was saying the Pledge of Allegiance. Others may also think I'm having chest pain, on the verge of a heart attack. I simply say that I'm fine, or laugh it off and move the conversation quickly to something else. It sometimes takes a concerted, conscious effort on my part at a dinner or other social engagement to keep my hands in front of me or at my sides so they are not touching or covering up some perceived defect.

3. ***The pants carousel.*** Women are stereotyped for trying on numerous outfits before they go out. It's part of a woman's mystique and appeal. But, of course, this doesn't apply to women only. We all want to look good in what we wear. Wanting to look our best is not BDD. It is normal. Occasionally feeling worried about how we look

compared to societal standards is also normal. But is it common for a person to try on dozens of outfits before going out at night? What about before leaving the house in the morning? What about trying on every pair of pants in the closet to make sure they all still fit as a daily routine, while getting ready for work? It doesn't happen every morning. It primarily happens when I have eaten a big meal the night before and gone to bed feeling full. I wake up feeling fat. The crazy thoughts about my body kick in, particularly my stomach and love handles. Then the compulsion to try on all my pants kicks in. If even one pair feels tight, it can send me into a depression.

4. ***A love/hate relationship with mirrors.*** Don't we all have that? Nothing out of the ordinary. The difference is that,, from adolescence into adulthood, I did not see my reflection when I looked into a mirror. I saw over-exaggerated love handles. A beach ball of a gut where none existed. A barely-receding hairline that looked like total baldness. A tiny zit that seemed to cover my entire face. The reflection in the mirror showed scarring that did not exist in real life. My chest seemed deformed and unattractive. I was even able to "see" stupidity. I saw a monster. Of course, these distorted perceptions never led me to avoid looking. In fact, I became

obsessed with mirrors, both drawn to them and terrified of them, like being unable to look away from a train wreck.

5. ***The hanging shirt.*** I hate to tuck in my shirts. Fortunately it has become kind of a style statement, so it does not seem too weird. For me, however, the untucked shirt is not an attempt to be stylish. The very act of tucking the shirt and creating less space between my stomach and my clothes is stressful for me. For years, I would avoid social events simply on the basis of whether I had to wear a suit or other clothes that required a tucked-in shirt. I would have rather been perceived as a slob than have to face perceived scrutiny of my waistline—even the imagined scrutiny from strangers and acquaintances.

6. ***Fear of social situations.*** This could be going to a party, nightclub, bar, or anywhere else that I expect people to be sizing each other up. Any situation where, in my mind, the entire scene is about judging and comparing my looks and "defects" to other people. The way I've coped with social anxiety has sometimes been worse than the anxiety itself. In the past, I'd often get drunk or high before an event. It was not unusual for me to drink half a pint of Jose Cuervo tequila

with a cocaine chaser before I went to a party or nightclub. And when the coke wears off? Confidence goes down. A cocaine baggie in one of my pockets was a mandatory accessory. I'd rarely wear my glasses or contacts. Out of vanity? No. For the blindness! As illogical as it sounds, if I couldn't see other people, then I wouldn't stress as much about whether they could see me. I still feel the pressure of the crowd these days, but I've learned to better cope with it (though I'll still leave the glasses at home from time to time . . .).

7. *Plans to artificially fix the "defects."* Any other BDD sufferers out there who have contemplated lap-band surgery even though they are at a healthy weight? A commercial for a bariatric weight-loss doctor comes on the television, advertising lap-band surgery. "Are you tired of dieting and worrying about weight loss?" Of course, I am. It has nothing to do with reality. I inevitably think, Hmmm . . . should I do that? Is now the time to have a silicone band wrapped permanently around my stomach? No ethical doctor would perform the surgery on me. But for a split second, my mind says something different. For that split second, I give in to my obsessive thoughts. Multiple visits to the plastic surgeon are common for BDD sufferers. I am no

exception. As of the writing of this book, I have had four hair transplants and one liposuction at a total cost of about $25,000. Not too extreme by BDD standards, but the only reason I did not have more procedures is because I could not rack up any more debt to get them.

8. ***Inner critic; outer critic.*** At my lowest points, I tend to see flaws not just in myself but in everyone I meet as well. When I obsess over defects in myself, zooming in 10X on even the most minute flaws, I can tend to do the same when I look at others. I am reflexively comparing them to me. Are my love handles or stomach worse or better? Do I have more or less hair? When I was younger, this sometimes turned me into what I despise—a bully.

The tics that I've described so far have not been life-threatening in themselves. These are behaviors that can be harmful, sure. Annoying, definitely. And when they occur frequently, they can be a sign that I need to take better control of my thought processes and work toward more positive everyday behavior. In the past, however, BDD has taken me to even darker places, to behaviors that can be very harmful or even fatal. For anyone who's experiencing any of the following actions or feelings, I recommend seeking help immediately.

1. **Self-medication.** Using drugs to try to change how you feel about yourself, how you see yourself, how you perceive others seeing you. I excelled in this. I've been an alcoholic. Cocaine addict. Abuser of weight-loss drugs, laxatives, and steroids. All of them gave me a brief self-image boost the moment I took them, but, in the end, they all led toward vicious cycles of destructive behavior.

2. **The extreme diet.** Eating disorders are something that many BDD sufferers are intimately familiar with. I am not an exception here, either. I have endured years-long bouts with both anorexia and bulimia. I was bulimic for decades. Eating disorders are fundamentally destructive to both mind and body.

3. **Depression.** Depression has always gone hand in hand with my BDD, and when it's at its worst, depression has robbed me of the will to live. Crying for no discernible reason almost every day. Sleeping up to fifteen hours a day. Not taking care of myself or my pets. What did I do to compensate for this? Binge and purge to control my weight and thoughts. Drink more alcohol. Take more drugs.

4. **Suicidal thoughts.** I am very lucky to be

above ground and here to write this book. I had a Spanish-made .45 automatic. I was ready to use it. I almost didn't make it.

For me, those four core self-destructive symptoms represented the steep drop into the abyss of BDD. The tics also played a part in that descent, to the extent I did not explore their origin and let them affect my ability to function day to day. The climb out of the hole was a long, slow, hard process. There were setbacks. There were times when it seemed easier to go backwards than forwards. There were times when simply giving up was within hand's reach. I forged ahead, baby step by baby step. Am I cured? That can mean different things to different people. I still have some obsessive-compulsive thoughts. There are BDD tics that have gotten less prominent as time goes on but still come and go. I am not happy all the time. No one is. Like everyone else, I have problems that cause stress and often depress me. Sometimes I still become confused about my path in life, only, now, I have the strength to face it. The strength to understand that I am not my distorted thoughts about my body. I am not defined by how I think others perceive me.

This book is about how I developed BDD and how it has affected my life. This book is also about how I have overcome BDD to lead a happy life, with confidence in my body and hope for the future. Through therapy, medication, and focused effort in shaping how my mind processes difficult experiences and negative thoughts, I have learned to manage addiction and other obsessive behaviors. I can now engage in social situations without dangerous crutches. I now understand that thoughts are not always reality. My body—fat or thin—no longer repulses me when I view it in the mirror. It is no longer my obsession.

Today, I'm free of eating disorders and addictions, except for my daily Starbucks Venti Blonde coffee. (In the world of addiction, the Venti seems a good trade-off from my old routine of coffee with a cocaine chaser to get going in the morning.) I can face the world of people and social interaction—with some stress, yes, but not life-disabling stress. Without the need to artificially change the image in the mirror. I love and am loved. I have been rejected and have recovered. I have let go. I have forgiven. I am alive. I am okay. You can be as well.

# CHAPTER 1:

## *The Last Days of Forbes Field*

*Thinking of Roberto Clemente.*

*M*y early years were no different than those of many children. I was not born with a distorted body image. Born January 11, 1961, I was the middle child of three brothers. We grew up near Pittsburgh, Pennsylvania, in a working-class town a bit removed from much of the turbulent social change that swept over the country in the '60s. My fragmented memories of my first nine years are of enjoyable birthday parties, winter sled riding with my brothers down the steep street where we lived, and our black German shepherd Hercules prowling the house, ready to scare off any monsters or bad guys I might have otherwise feared.

My grandparents on both sides were Jewish immigrants who escaped persecution in the former Soviet Union and Romania by boarding boats headed for Ellis Island. My grandfather on my father's side had a grocery store in New Jersey for a while and then sold groceries out of the back of his truck in Pittsburgh. He died when I was five. I have no memories of him. I do recall my father once walking up the stairs from our basement holding lit candles. When I asked my mom why he was holding them, she told me my grandfather had died. For many years, I could remember the sound of my father's footsteps coming up those stairs, bringing with him something silent, mysterious, and sad.

*Grandfather Fred and my "Nanny."*

My maternal grandfather sold socks, ties, and other men's sundries door to door to businesses in Pittsburgh. As a child, I enjoyed going through the big brown trunk he kept under his bed that was full of clothing samples. They smelled of city air and dusty pavement, of my grandfather's trek from store to store, which he made day after day to pay the rent on my grandparents' small apartment in Squirrel Hill. Who bought those clothes? I never knew.

Like me, my father was the middle of three brothers. He earned a trade-school education, fought in World War II and the Korean War, and operated a "trim shop" with his older brother in the same location in Pittsburgh for almost fifty years. A trim shop is a garage that specializes in adding extra features to cars—folks would bring in their vehicles to get a convertible roof put on, seats reupholstered, or have one of those giant "pimp wheel" continental kit tire-compartments fixed onto the back of their Cadillacs. Though my younger brother worked there for one summer, none of us elected to go into the family business. Our father didn't want that for us, anyway. Like many fathers, his dream was for us to get an education and strike out on our own. He didn't want us to have what he had. He wanted us to have it all.

My father instilled in us the values he'd acquired as the middle of three sons. Stay close as brothers. Never forget or abandon family. He made sure all of us had the opportunity to attain college degrees, and we all did. I attended the Pennsylvania State University. I went on to get a law degree from the University of Pittsburgh. My older brother Mark is a well-known entrepreneur and sports-franchise owner. My younger brother Jeff is a successful media executive.

Growing up, we attended summer camps, took family trips to the Catskills, shoveled snow from driveways for spending money, collected baseball cards, and went to Pittsburgh Pirates baseball games. I loved baseball growing up. In 1969, when I was eight years old, my father took me and my brothers to Forbes Field to see the Pittsburgh Pirates play the Miracle New York Mets. It's the first baseball game I have memories of attending. I recall a sunny Sunday afternoon, sitting in stands not far from home plate. I remember the smell of hot dogs, popcorn, and my father's aftershave. And I remember the security of love and family in that moment. I had no self-doubts, no fears. Thirty-one years later, I would honor the memory of that day with a brick for my father at the Pirates' brand-new stadium, PNC Park. It's still there today. To My Father, A True Buccos Fan.

As I got older, I'd go to Pirates games with my brothers. We would take the bus into town and walk across the Allegheny River to Three Rivers Stadium. Once in a while, we would bribe a stadium guard with a corned beef sandwich to let us sit in better seats. Sometimes we'd go to doubleheaders and get ticket stubs for good seats from people who could not stay for the second game. It was always sunny and hot with the smell of popcorn and hot dogs in the air—to a child, the smells of heaven. It was at those games, sitting with my father or brothers, that I came to understand the sort of man I wanted to become.

My brothers and I had a weekly ritual of visiting a local mom-and-pop store called Gracie's, which sold baseball cards and other novelties. I always hoped to find a Willie Stargell or Roberto Clemente card hidden in my new pack. Willie Stargell was a Pittsburgh icon who began his storied, twenty-year career with the Pirates when I was just a baby. I grew up in awe of his legendary power—he'd swing a sledgehammer in the batter's box to warm up, and then he'd launch baseballs right out of the park. Willie was a hero, but it was Roberto Clemente who was my true idol.

Clemente was a sportsman and a humanitarian, but, as a child, I had no idea who Roberto Clemente was as a person. I never met him. It didn't matter. I wanted the glory that he represented. In my mind, stardom was the crowning achievement of growing up and becoming an adult. That's what I wanted more than anything else. To me, Roberto Clemente was a Pittsburgh hero loved by all. I wanted that for myself.

Of course, I gave baseball a shot, playing Little League. On the field, I was a little more Willie Stargell than Roberto Clemente: I was nearing 200 pounds before I was twelve, but, at the plate, my weight was an asset, not a defect. I relished the feeling of power. I hit a grand slam in my very first Little League game. I was on top of the world when I was mobbed by my teammates crossing home plate. Unfortunately, I was not a very good fielder. We lost the game. My error at second base and wild throw home allowed the winning run to score.

When I am back in Pittsburgh and I go by that field, I can play the scene in my mind like a movie. Bases loaded. The pitch. The long fly ball to left. Not realizing I had hit a grand slam until I ran into the arms of my teammates. For that one moment in time, my self-consciousness about my weight, my early feelings of shyness and isolation were gone. I was accepted. I had risen above it all—for a moment. I wish I could have bottled that moment.

My baseball "career" ended not long after it began. It was not because of injury or lack of interest. The coach announced in front of the entire team during a practice that I would run faster if I "pretended I was chasing a refrigerator to first base." It got a good laugh from my teammates, and the coach laughed, too. I was humiliated. This was becoming a normal occurrence with schoolmates, but, this time, the cause of my embarrassment was an adult. In a moment, I had gone from being revered as a power hitter to being called out for what I really was: a fat slob. The illusion was no more.

A couple years later, dreams of baseball stardom would end for good. It was December 31, 1972.

My parents had gone to a New Year's Eve party. My grandfather Fred was babysitting me. I had stayed up watching TV late into the 1973 New Year's morning. I watched a flick called *It Grows on Trees*. I remember being fascinated with the fantasy that money could grow on trees. Money growing on trees seemed a simple solution to so many complex problems.

The next morning, my grandfather walked into the kitchen as I was eating my cereal. In his deep voice, ravaged by a stroke years before, he told me that Roberto Clemente had been killed in a plane crash overnight. I didn't believe him. I rushed to the television and heard the news I would never forget. My baseball hero's plane had gone down. I would hold out hope that he would be found alive: the hope of an eleven-year-old who did not understand that it would be practically impossible for anyone to survive an airplane crash over the ocean. I told myself Roberto would be found. I glued myself to the television all day, waiting for news of his rescue at sea, news that would never come. With Clemente's death something of that sense of safety, of security, of uncomplicated happiness of the sort experienced at the ball field was lost as well. I felt that, with the death of my hero, a part of me died. I felt alone and isolated. Who would I grow up to become, now that I didn't have the example of my idol?

•

Spring, 1971. I distinctly remember the soundtrack of my first crush. Her name was Sarah, and we were assigned to work on a project about Israel together in fourth grade. Or, I should say, I schemed my hardest and made sure I was assigned to work with her. That year the song that played in my head on repeat was Peter, Paul, and Mary's version of "Leaving on a Jet Plane." Our teacher played it in class one day, and I'd hear the song all over again every time I saw Sarah.

*Dream about the days to come*
*When I won't have to leave alone*

I was always brutally shy, but not always overweight. I started to add a lot of weight that year, when my family moved from Scott Township to the more upper-class Mt. Lebanon. Both are southern suburbs of Pittsburgh. It was the next step up the social ladder that many living in Scott had made. I was excited about relocating because so many of my friends from my old school had made the exact same move a couple years before. But I was sad to leave some of my other friends behind. The very last day at Nixon Elementary, after we got off the bus, my close friend Robert handed me a picture of himself along with a dime (the cost of a pay-phone call back then) and told me not to forget him. We hugged. I never saw him again. I walked a mile to my new home and new life.

After we'd settled in at Mt. Lebanon, I would play Peter, Paul, and Mary on my parents' record player and feel alone and helpless, scared to reach out to make new friends. Though I knew kids in Mt. Lebanon from my old school, new cliques had formed, and I was on the outside. What does a chubby ten-year-old do when he feels ostracized and depressed? I ate. I gained weight. My body changed in a way that made me ashamed. It was during this time that I distinctly remember feeling that I was ugly and different. Somehow defective. Still, I thought that if only I could reach out to Sarah, I could find someone to share my secrets with, someone who would care.

*So kiss me and smile for me . . .*

Isn't that what every little boy wants when he experiences his first romantic feelings and is trying to understand them? He wants his hand held, that warm, palm-to-palm feeling. The puppy-love butterflies in his stomach. He wants a kiss.

*Hold me like you'll never let me go . . .*

My project with Sarah didn't work out as I'd hoped. We'd sit together, and music would swell in my heart. But no words would come out of my mouth. Literally. I just sat there next to her, trying to think of the words that would win her loyalty and affection, and none would come. Eventually, she was so unnerved by the experience that she asked to be assigned a new partner. I was crushed.

To this day, the words from "Leaving on a Jet Plane" reverberate in my heart and take me back to that innocent time of yearning to have Sarah hold my hand.

•

Heroes can be sports starts or movie stars or rock stars, but heroes can also be family members who provide a sense of home, of safety. As a child, I did not grasp the concept that hard work was required to provide for a family, but I knew my father took care of me. He cooked me his special chili made with Sloppy Joe Sauce. He made me salads from his personal recipe. I still make them today: lettuce, tuna fish, relish, black olives, and mayo. He would mix them together in a large, shiny, stainless steel bowl. When we were old enough, he always made sure I had a car to drive. Some of the cars were one step from the scrap heap, but they always ran. And, for a teenager, having bad transportation was better than having no transportation. Having a car when many other kids didn't earned me a base level of acceptance, which I would take any way I could get it. My father also told me everything was okay, and he held me when I was overcome with the daily build-up of shame. Reflected in my father's gaze, I was still a good kid. A kid worthy of love.

After our move to Mt. Lebanon, I remember once admitting to him that I'd been stealing change from his giant jar of quarters every day while he was at work. My friend would bounce a basketball on the wooden floor in my father's bedroom so no one could hear the change in the jar jingle as I filled my pockets. I spent the ill-gotten money on baseball cards, still hoping to find a Clemente or Stargell card in the deck. I thought the deed was worthy of expulsion from the family, and I felt the kind of burning guilt that would later become familiar. He never caught me doing it. He didn't need to. The guilt became so intense that I broke down bawling and told him. My father did not need to scold or discipline me. He knew how the overwhelming guilt affected me, and he knew I wouldn't do it again. He only needed to hold me, which is what he did. He gave me a sense of safety and fair play. My father provided confidence that let me know I could go to bed, assured he would also be there for me the next day, and the day after that.

By 1971, I already had a pretty clear idea of how I wanted to be perceived when I grew up. I wanted to be admired like my hero, Roberto Clemente. I wanted to be cool as a rock star, able to attract friends and find adventure and serenade pretty girls. And I wanted to be an honest, caring, hard-working man, the sort of man I saw in my father. But, by 1971, I also felt something was deeply wrong. I was painfully shy and had trouble connecting with classmates, especially the kids at my new school. I was big and getting bigger, learning to compensate for stress and disappointment by binging on Chef Boyardee ravioli. And I frequently felt that I was already failing to measure up. While there was no diagnosis, looking back, I believe that a level of depression had taken root in adolescence that would stay with me for the rest of my life.

According to BDD researchers, signs and symptoms of body dysmorphia, including depression, often first start to emerge in adolescence. In that respect, my experience was not unique. It is in early adolescence that we usually have our first experiences with bullying, broken relationships (whether it's a grade-school crush or family discord), or other traumas that compound and trigger any innate tendencies toward obsessive behavior. It is in early adolescence that our minds become steeped in hormones that transform who we are and how we relate to the world. And it is in early adolescence that we start to form a defined sense of self-image.

•

Summer, 1971. I'm at Emma Kaufmann Camp near Morgantown, West Virginia. Emma Kaufmann is a summer tradition for countless Jewish children from Pittsburgh and elsewhere, and it was a yearly tradition in our family.

It is the night of the Emma Kaufmann Camp talent show. I walk up to the front of the stage. I sweat a little more with each creak of the old wooden boards. I turn and face a hundred ten- and eleven-year-olds. They are laughing and joking with each other. In my mind, they are making fun of me. I am terrified. Every eye seems to be focused on my excessive girth. I am nervous and nauseous, my teeth grinding. The musty smell of the wood-frame building seems suffocating. Rain patters on the leaves outside.

The Beatles hit "Let It Be" is the song. There's no microphone and no music. I am standing exposed and vulnerable in front of a hundred other kids. I remind myself that this was my choice. I chose to sing this song, nobody was making me, and I chose to sing because I wanted to take control of my fear. To cast aside uncertainty. To become popular. To be noticed. If I could sing "Let It Be," my weight would not matter. My shyness would not matter. I hoped this would be no different from a piano recital. I could handle those; I could handle this. Take a deep breath. Count to ten. Focus on a fixed point. In recitals, I focused on the piano keys. At camp, I now focus on the wooden floor in front of me. I am too frightened to look at the kids staring at me, talking and laughing. I open my mouth. The only sound that emerges is a guttural groan, the sound a wounded animal might make.

I start to sweat more. Kids are laughing. Now I'm sure they are laughing at me. I'm humiliated—not much different than the humiliation of shyness and the body-oriented shame that constantly gripped me, but this time the feeling is intensified, like a magnifying glass focusing sunlight on a blade of grass.

Continuing to concentrate on the wooden floor, I walk off the stage and move quickly through the door. I break into a run and bolt back to my empty cabin. I sob, knowing that the worst is yet to come. My cabin mates will be back soon. Some are just waiting for the next excuse to ridicule me, as if bored with calling me "fat." Our cabin counselor will intervene and tell them to leave me alone, as he had done before. I want to go home, but I can't.

My fellow campers filter back into the cabin. One makes his way straight for me as I lie on my bunk. "Not only are you fat, but you sing like shit," he says. Still crying, I jump up and attack him. I run at him as hard as I can and use all of my 200 pounds to knock him back onto the bed. I've stood up for myself. It feels good.

The bully of Emma Kaufmann will never bother me again, but I end up banned from the Camper vs. Counselor softball game, the one event where I would feel comfortable around my peers.

The talent show was just the beginning of my embarrassments. At Emma Kaufmann, I had a camp crush. I remember her standing on the porch of her cabin, her smile bright against her Mediterranean skin and her dark, flowing hair. I would make any excuse I could to get within feet of her during various camp activities. I tried to befriend her friends in order to be near her. But no matter how close I got, I was unable to say anything other than mumbled "hello" as I looked at the ground. She sometimes smiled and hello-ed back, but that was as far as we'd get. And I remember her laughing derisively at the unwanted and embarrassing shout from my friend that I had a crush on her.

Man, I hated camp.

Just prior to the end of my stay at Emma Kaufmann, another boy in the cabin approached me. He knew I wanted to be included in something. Even crime would do. We planned to steal five bucks from the boy I had fought after the talent show. When our cabin mates were gone, we crept through the darkness of the empty barracks and took the money.

Kids were questioned. Our counselor yelled. I was terrified my co-conspirator would turn me in. I was an easy target. A guilty target. The fat, reclusive kid who croaked when he tried to sing. But the other boy stayed silent, and I spent the $2.50 on candy. More than forty years later, I can still remember how my stomach knotted up as I handed over my ill-gotten gains to the store clerk to buy Red Hots, Jaw Breakers, and Juicy Fruit gum. I could feel that my camp mates, the clerk, the camp counselor, and everyone in the store knew I was a thief and an outcast. I was horrified when the camp counselor began interrogating everyone over the theft. His final words on the subject: "I guess some jerk is five dollars richer." I was that jerk. I agreed with him.

It's the last night of camp. I am alone on the fringes of the campfire on a cool summer evening. Kids are singing the camp songs.

*Sit by the fire, stay close as the air*
*Sharing our memories of camp*
*The beauty of the woods*
*The coolness of the water in the lake*
*We share together . . .*

Too embarrassed from my talent-show debacle to sing along, I can't identify with any of it. There's no sharing; I feel no beauty. The words only intensify my feelings of loneliness and isolation.

The other campers are practicing the time-honored tradition of telling camp horror stories, about the one-armed hook men who will kill us in our sleep, or about daring each other to drink bug juice. The smell of toasting marshmallows, wet burning wood, and leaves permeate the air. Kids who had found their camp loves are holding hands, kissing, and cuddling.

I'm doing none of that. I'm in the cold grass on

the fringes. I want to be closer to the heat; I want to fit in. That sense of being ostracized would later become familiar to me as an alcoholic. Being drunk often makes you an outsider in social situations — either in reality or just in your head.

The way I imagined that those other kids saw me left an indelible imprint on my self-image. The great thing about attending camp in the West Virginia woods was that there were no mirrors. The bad thing was that other children acted as mirrors.

Of course, having a hard time at summer camp and experiencing social frustrations are hardly rare in adolescence. Many children suffer even greater indignities and don't grow up to spend entire mornings trying on every pair of pants they own. Kids who endured heartbreak don't always grow up and seek out plastic surgery to fix nonexistent flaws. I sometimes wonder — had my life had been just slightly different — if I, too, could look back on Emma Kaufmann Camp and laugh about my awkward years instead of reliving them in painful detail. The traumas and hurt feelings of childhood could have slipped away, regardless of their severity. But they didn't. The traumas—big and small—stayed with me and grew into deeply obsessive and self-destructive thoughts as I became more and more uncomfortable with the person I saw in the mirror.

Decades later, one of the most important steps I took in recovery was to get honest about those experiences. I approached the shy child and assured him that everything is okay. I told the young Brian that's the way things are when you're growing up. I told him that he doesn't need to become a Clemente, or even his own father. He need only become the happiest possible version of himself.

# CHAPTER 2:
## *Shy, Fat, and Bullied*

*Throwing my weight around with my brother Jeff.*

W hen I was thirteen years old, I was "pantsed" by kids who I thought were my friends. Or should I say, I was pantsed by kids who I was pretending were my friends in a vain attempt to feel accepted. It was the most humiliating experience of my young life. In reality, it was a physical assault.

While I was walking home from junior high with these classmates, they started making fun of the shiny gold pants my brother Mark had given me, commenting on how tightly they fit my fat body. They started pulling at them. One kid yanked them down over my underwear and tore them off me. The rest joined in ripping them to pieces, which they threw into the street. Then they laughed and taunted me about having to walk the mile home on a busy street in my underwear. Many drivers passed and gawked, but no one stopped to help. I gathered up the shreds of my pants and tried to cover myself up for the walk home—a cross-country trek of shame. The message from my "friends" was loud and clear: I was not one of them. As they walked away, the last thing they said was, "Hey, Cuban, when you get some new pants, get a bra while you're at it."

What happened that day was not posted on You-Tube. No Facebook page was created. No one tweeted about it. There was no Facebook. There was no Internet. There was no such thing as cyber-bullying in 1974. It never went beyond the group involved and whomever they boasted to about their deeds. Instead, bullying went "viral" by spreading through the cafeteria and classroom. After the incident, kids would come up to me in the lunch line and ask me how I liked walking home in my underwear. I could feel their derisive looks and smirks. But I didn't fight back as I had done in summer camp. Instead, I used my tried and true technique of self-deprecating humor and self-degradation—a coping skill I would take with me into adulthood. "Ha, they really got me good, didn't they. . . ." Instead of fighting back or getting angry, it seemed easier to make fun of myself and try to be everyone's friend, even if they continued to bully me.

I never stood up for myself, so nothing happened. I could have fought back. I could have gone to my parents. I could have gone to the school. I did none of those things. Thinking back, it seems clear that it was because I was ashamed. I was ashamed of my body, and I agreed with the kids who were humiliating me. I felt it was right that I should be humiliated by my inability to control my body. What I saw in the mirror was a mass of grotesque imperfections, and the bullies had done me the favor of confirming that my thoughts about myself were accurate.

For some kids, the Episode of the Gold Pants might seem like a typical rite of passage, an act of mortification that they might even laugh about as adults. But, for me, the walk of shame and the public gossip that followed it altered how I thought about myself for many long years. How is that possible? Why did this one act of bullying have such an outsized impact on my psyche? Bullying is a hot topic in the media now, with new books released every season about the deleterious effects of bullying culture on kids throughout the country. We all read news reports about children pushed to acts of self-harm by elaborately orchestrated bullying campaigns. The subject has been covered so extensively lately that there's even a sort of backlash: a few writers point out that some of what we label "bullying" is an inevitable part of the fabric of childhood and that over-diagnosing the problem is counterproductive.

What some of these conversations miss, however, is that all bullies and their victims are individuals with rich and complex personalities, not just generic social actors. To every experience, we all bring unique, innate tendencies, along with a network of past experiences. In my case, I already had an innate tendency toward obsessive behavior and shyness, a growing sense of social isolation in a new school environment, and—perhaps as significant as anything—a home life increasingly characterized by discord and verbal abuse from my mom. At school, I badly wanted to fit in, and I lived in constant fear that I'd hear from my peers words that echoed those I'd hear from my mother at home: We don't accept fat pigs and dumb bunnies into our group.

•

My relationship with my mother was complicated and sometimes verbally volatile. She was battling demons in her relationship with her own mother, and, starting in my early teens—when I began to put on more weight—she started to take her stress out on me. She'd belittle my physical appearance and intellectual abilities. "Why are you such a dumb bunny?" she'd wonder when I'd forget to do something. "You're going to grow up to be a fat pig if you keep eating like that," she'd warn when she would come home at lunch and see me enjoying my favorite Chef Boyardee ravioli or Beefaroni. My mother had deep insecurities of her own as an adult and struggled through them, but her problems took different forms, and she found her own sources of comfort.

*My mom is happy I finished the Pittsburgh Marathon. So am I!*

Fall, 1972. Downstairs with my friends listening to records. "Roundabout" by the musical group Yes and "Monster Mash" are making us laugh. My friend Alex is annoying the hell out of us. He's dancing while holding a bowl of Chef Boyardee spaghetti and singing with his mouth open. I cringe every time a piece of spaghetti launches from his mouth onto my parents' polished wooden floor. "That's just the way I chew!" he exclaims.

*I'll be the roundabout*

— A blood-curdling scream comes from upstairs.

*The words will make you out 'n' out*

—and then a prolonged screech.

It's not from Alex. It's not from the song playing on the stereo in our living room. There's no psychotic intruder in our home. It's my mom. She's upstairs, sitting in a closet, screaming into her pillow. 'She's trying out primal therapy, a type of self-help treatment. The incredible embarrassment! What does an eleven-year-old boy say to his friends about his mother when he does not understand her himself? I shrugged it off with no explanation and herded my friends outside, angry at my mom for thinking only of herself. Primal therapy was popular in the early '70s. It was created by psychotherapist Arthur Janov, who believed that re-experiencing childhood trauma and then expressing the pain of it (hence the screaming) would relieve emotional distress—of which my mom certainly had her share. I can't blame her for going into a closet and screaming. Notable people who dabbled in primal therapy include John Lennon and Steve Jobs. Primal therapy was like many faddish self-help, pop-psychology movements that have emerged over the decades. They may bring comfort, but, like all trends, they come and go, and often leave people who have ingrained mental-health challenges still searching for answers.

Throughout my life, I've experimented with my

share of self-help du jour. As an adult, during my darkest episodes of body dysmorphia, depression, and addiction, I'd do my share of therapeutic screaming as part of a greater pattern of tension-relief rituals. I'd even go as far as self-harm, punching myself repeatedly in the face when I felt I had been a "dumb bunny." Each bruising punch temporarily dulled the shame of body and mind, and the resultant pain was a reminder of that fat little boy I used to be. Even so, my OCD told me I needed to punch more often, and harder.

My mom was no different than I was in my thirties and forties. A troubled person, in pain from her childhood, looking for answers. She, like me, wanted to be loved by a mother who was also in conflict. She did not engage in extreme eating behaviors, do cocaine, or abuse alcohol. She acted out her anger at her mother. She screamed in a closet. She screamed at me. She underwent therapy. Searching for something, anything, to maintain an even keel. She, like me, had a mother who would tell her she was too fat. My grandmother had her own psychological issues, perhaps including obsessive-compulsive disorder or even, according to my mother, schizophrenia. When I look at the behavioral history running down through our generations, it would seem to lend credence to the notion that there is a genetic component to BDD. But of course, traumatic experiences can be passed through the generations as well.

My grandmother came to the United States at eighteen years old, speaking no English. She led the difficult life of a Russian immigrant, living in housing projects, surviving on the barest resources. She struggled to better her life against long odds, and she succeeded. My mother took on the traditional roles of a wife in mid-twentieth-century America, and she eventually managed to find a healthy identity. She sold books and real estate. She obtained her college degree later in life. She became a drug and alcohol counselor. I am very proud of my mom's ability to force her way through the pain of a rough childhood and create a viable life for herself—an ability I could not find in myself for many years. Shame is a monstrous cliff to climb.

But, as a child, I didn't understand my mother as a person who had her own challenges, her own difficult past. It was easier to retreat to my bedroom, and put my own pillow over my head to muffle her screams. It became about me. Was I making her do this? What about me made her want to do that? Because I was fat? Because I was stupid? I didn't get it. I wanted her to pay attention to me and not scream in a closet.

Of course, she did give me motherly support. She took me to piano lessons. She took me swimming. She was there when I was sick. So, why do the bad times stand out more? Probably because they were traumatic and generated the strongest feelings.

*The solace of a child's bedroom.*

My memory is not the best gauge of our relationship; all I really have are the feelings and mental snapshots of painful moments. Dredging through all those memories and trying to pinpoint the origins of my unhealthy thoughts, I am left with this conclusion: It is so important to talk to your children about their hopes, fears, and failures. They have them. It is even more important to choose your words carefully when you have those discussions. If you need help, there are all kinds of options available today that did not exist when I was a child. It's a different era. You may not see the impact of hurtful words immediately. Bullying causes pain that builds in a child like in a pressure cooker. Sooner or later, that steam has to find its way out. It may be while your child is living at home, or it may be years or even decades later.

•

Summer, 1973. Once or twice a month, I would take a twelve-mile bus ride—sometimes alone, sometimes with my brothers—to visit my beloved grandmother, Sarah, who I called "Nanny." She lived in Squirrel Hill, a predominantly Jewish neighborhood in Pittsburgh. If my brothers came along, we would watch cartoons and The Three Stooges. We would "flip" baseball cards that we had bought with the money Nanny had given us—one of us would throw a card in the air, and if it landed face up, the winner could claim one of the other brothers' new cards. When Nanny was not in the room, my grandfather would pull ten-dollar bills out of the Bible he kept on the nightstand and make me promise not to tell Nanny where his stash was.

Many days, Nanny and I would take the bus to Kennywood, Pittsburgh's amusement park. It smelled of popcorn and cotton candy. Nanny would give me money to spend on food and rides. She would find a bench under a shady tree and sit for hours without a book, radio, or anything to make the time pass more quickly, while I rode the rides and roamed the park. I would come back to her bench for the baloney sandwich with white bread and yellow mustard that she had packed for my lunch. She would hug me fiercely, as though she hadn't seen me in years. Sometimes when I think back on those moments, I can still taste the sandwich and feel the sun dappling my skin. After lunch, she would give me more money for rides, and, when I was worn out, we would take the bus home. I have often wondered what she thought about while she sat alone, waiting for me. Was it memories of the old world? Was it her troubled relationship with her daughter—my mother?

My Nanny loved her grandkids. From my childhood point of view, she also loved her only child. Unfortunately, it was not a good relationship while I was growing up. There was a lot of yelling. Nanny would call the house multiple times a day, often in quick succession. My mother would hang up on her. If I answered, my mother would refuse to take the call and make me deal with it instead. This drove Nanny to tears, and she would ask in her heavy Russian accent, "Why won't your mother talk to me? Please get her to talk to me! Why does she hate me? Why does your mother yell at me?"

I had no answers for her. I would beg my mother to take the phone. Eventually I started hanging up on her myself—my Nanny, who only wanted to hear the voices of her daughter and grandchildren. Sometimes Nanny would make the long bus trip to our house, only to be turned away at the door. I was forbidden to let her in. She would stand outside the door in tears, until she would finally go home. As a child, I could not possibly understand the depths of anger my mother had, or the complicated history that led to the drama I witnessed. Still, their fighting broke my heart. I cried often. I hated myself for being unable to make my grandmother happy, to repair her relationship with her daughter. I hated my mother for the way she treated my Nanny and for causing me to hate Nanny. Only a monster would ignore his weeping grandmother like that—but I was that monster.

I began to avoid my grandmother. I couldn't handle the strange family dynamics I'd become a part of. I ended up not seeing her for years. She died in 1988. She had been living in a senior citizens home. I got a short phone call from my mother, informing me that she had died. I cried selfishly for never saying goodbye and for my shortcomings in not standing up for her. I still cry over it today. Recovery does not mean the abdication of emotion.

•

Summer, 1975. While my relationships at home foundered and my friendships at school remained rocky, I was still moving further away from the person I'd wanted to become. Not only was I bullied, I occasionally played the bully. Under pressure to fit in, I could sink to real acts of cruelty, such as killing a bird on a dare. I was standing in my driveway with two neighborhood kids. They egged me on to shoot, to test out my cool new pellet gun. I could have said no. I didn't.

Pellet rifle with scope focused in, I closed my eyes and pulled the trigger. There was a strong burst of air and the thwack of the pellet cutting through leaves. Then the sickening thud as the pellet struck the unsuspecting bird. It fell to the driveway, flailing its wings and writhing. My friends laughed and congratulated me on a good shot. I was nauseated by what I had done. I wanted to cry, but I couldn't. I would be called a "pussy" and ostracized. I had to pretend that I was relishing this bloody act and bonding with my friends. I wanted to put the robin out of its suffering, but I could not bring myself to approach the dying creature. Instead I walked away, joining in my friends' enjoyment of my prowess with forced laughter. I did not want to harm a living creature. I just wanted to be accepted, wanted it so badly I was willing to kill gratuitously. When I got up to my bedroom, I wept. I could still see the robin writhing on the driveway. I ran back outside, but it had already died. I nudged it behind a tree so I wouldn't have to see it and be reminded of my weakness and cruelty. All these years later, I can still see that bird falling from the tree. Some images and feelings of guilt are so ingrained I may take them to my grave.

•

Fall, 1976. My mother and father were going through a difficult time. Divorce seemed imminent. Out of their conflict, a moment arose in which I was briefly in tune with my mother's feelings of grief and helplessness. It was a transcendent experience for me as a teen, because I forgot about my feelings of self-hatred and helplessness and realized that my mom had similar feelings about herself.

My mother had made plans to take me and my brother Jeff to Disney World by bus. Naturally, I was excited. About two weeks before we were supposed to go, my mother and I were in our basement. She told me that she and my father would be getting divorced and that we would be unable to afford to go. She started crying. All of my hateful, painful thoughts about how she viewed me disappeared. All I knew at that moment was that I loved my mom deeply. I felt her heartache as if it were my own. I told her that no matter what happened, I loved her and my father. I wouldn't take sides. I was the child of them both.

My parents never did divorce.

Coming to terms with my relationship with my mother has been extremely important in recovering from my body dysmorphic issues. For me, overcoming BDD has required getting honest about the past—including forgiving the people who hurt me. When I was able to do that, I was more able to live in the present. My mother's pain was not about me, even if it was sometimes taken out on me. It has taken me my whole life to understand that. How did I get there? There's no "one size fits all" road map.

One thing is universal, however. People do not just suddenly start looking at themselves in a new way. The brain does not instantly compile a whole image from a shattered one. Just as breaking down the past is a gradual process, rebuilding is a process as well. It's a journey of self-discovery, adjustment, and recognition of the challenges faced by loved ones.

My own battle to find real solace and mental health was just beginning. By sixteen, I was already exhibiting some of the early signs of BDD, the first odd tics that would become compulsions later in life. One of the first tics I can remember is the fear of taking my shirt off and exposing my stomach. I always wore loose clothing to conceal my gut. I vividly remember my embarrassment at the swimming pool and in high-school gym class—the phrase "shirts and skins" still evokes childhood shame. I would cringe every time the gym teach bellowed, "WE'RE PLAYING BASKETBALL TODAY, SHIRTS AND SKINS! SHIRTS OFF!"

The words "shirts and skins"—meaning one team wore shirts and the other didn't—sent me into a paralyzed state. I could only imagine what the other kids thought when they actually saw my excessive fat, my gut hanging over my shorts. Every boy and girl in the gym was a mirror of my self-disgust. Of course, I had no idea what they were really thinking. What I did know, however, was how I felt looking at myself. I avoided the locker room, always changing in private or at home.

If I knew that there was going to be a basketball

game or other gym activity that meant I might get chosen for skins, I would sometimes fake illness to be excused from gym or skip school altogether. I had no desire for anyone in the world to see me without my shirt on. Then came the comments from my gym teacher that I needed to lose some weight. Comments made in front of the other students. I hated gym. But my shame there was relatively mild compared to other teenage humiliations.

Spring, 1977. Then there were girls. At sixteen, I worked up the nerve to attend my first high-school dance. A Sadie Hawkins dance was scheduled for the Mt. Lebanon High School gymnasium. The Sadie Hawkins tradition is that girls invite boys, though, as usual, nobody invited me that year. I had to find rare reserves of courage even to go alone. The dance was a scene right out of the movie *Sixteen Candles*, with me moping in the gym bleachers with the John Cusacks and Anthony Michael Halls of Mt. Lebanon Senior High. We stood there watching the kids with dates who were holding hands, dancing, laughing, and talking about where they were going to hang out after the dance. I scrutinized every guy with a girl I considered pretty and tried to analyze what it took to be that guy. What could I change?

As I stood there wishing I were one of the kids dancing, one of the prettier girls made eye contact with me. She started walking toward me. I began to sweat. Someone was interested in me! By the time she came face to face with me, I was a damp, heart-pounding mess. I remember her raven hair—and the sneer of disdain on her face as she said, "Do you always hold your brother's hand when you walk with him? You're pretty weird." She was referring to a couple days before, when I had walked my little brother Jeff home from school while holding his hand.

I love my brothers. My father instilled a sense of loyalty between us when we were very young. Always comfort and protect each other in times of need. I certainly didn't think holding my brother's hand was weird. I just wanted him to feel safe.

The dark-haired beauty and her friends giggled and walked away, and left me standing there with my raging self-doubt. I blended back into the bleachers of the gymnasium and then set out into the night to walk home, back up that same hill I where I had held my brother's hand. I never attended another high-school social function.

Of course, what she said was nothing exceptionally cruel. It would seem relatively benign by contemporary bullying standards. But I remember the scene word for word and every feature on the young girl's face like it was yesterday. I wonder how she turned out. No doubt she went on to college, met the guy of her dreams, had kids and maybe even grandkids. She would not remember that moment. She probably would not have remembered it six months later. We are all different in how we process our thoughts and feelings. In today's world, with the advent of social media, I often wonder what bullied children will look like in their later years, and how episodes of bullying will guide their image of themselves as they grow. Will they survive to fifty? Studies show that body dysmorphic disorder increases the chances of suicide in teens. How many will channel this judgment by their peers into eating disorders, drug addiction, or even worse? If my experience was any guide, BDD sufferers remain silent, unsure how to articulate out-of-control feelings, with parents often ill-equipped to understand them. Of all the ways that BDD can send lives off track, the silence bred from shame can be the most dangerous symptom of all. When young people are silent in the face of public bullying, that's when loved ones need to step in.

•

Winter Break, 1978. A road trip from Pittsburgh to Fort Lauderdale, Florida with my brother Mark! When my parents told me that he would be taking me, I was ecstatic. We borrowed my mom's big brown Cadillac Coupe de Ville and drove straight down. It was the year of Saturday Night Fever. The disco craze was in high gear. We were jamming the soundtrack the entire trip. There was also a lot of Barry Manilow going on. The song "Daybreak" seemed to be playing quite a bit. It was a great bonding time. Our time in

Fort Lauderdale was spent going to the beach, listening to the Bee Gees, and playing pinball. I couldn't go to the clubs with Mark because I was not eighteen, but we spent time together and had fun. When we were not together, I ate a lot of Burger King Whoppers while playing pinball. At this point, food was

*Thinking of Burger King and Saturday Night Fever.*

a crutch I used to make myself feel better when depressed. The trip ended on a sour note when I was mugged at knife-point by a kid who had befriended me at the Pinball Palace next to our hotel. I never told my brother about it. I never told my parents. Why risk being thought of as a bigger loser than I already viewed myself? I thought.

I don't want to give the impression that I was friendless. I did forge some bonds with some kids who were like me, shy and on the outside of the "cool kid" circles. I sometimes went on backpacking trips with my closest high-school friend, who was also a fringe-dweller. We would go to the Allegheny Mountains in the dead of winter with our rented gear, some marijuana, and bottles of Southern Comfort Whiskey. We'd get drunk, smoke pot by the fire, and make fun of the groups I wanted so badly to be a part of.

By my senior year of high school, my fate seemed set. I had ballooned to 250 pounds and rising. Eating was my drug. I obsessed over my weight and was horrified by my appearance. This caused me to eat even more: a vicious cycle. Depression had long since set in. I had no respect for myself in terms of my health or achievements and saw no reason to do anything to change. I had begun skipping school regularly to get drunk and smoke pot in the woods with my friends. The drinking age in Pennsylvania was twenty-one. It was eighteen in the neighboring states of West Virginia and Ohio. Both were no more than an hour's drive. We would skip school and road trip with our fake IDs over the state line and stock up on 3.2 beer and liquor. We would bring it back and hide it in the woods. Drinking and getting high were magic spells that could briefly make me feel accepted and forget the monster I saw when I looked in the mirror.

Then high school ended, and it was time to go to college. I could not wait to walk out those doors of Mt. Lebanon High for the last time. All I felt was anger over my four years of loneliness and isolation. I had no desire to excel in higher education, but I did have a desire to get away from my mother. I was not staying in Pittsburgh. Mark attended Indiana University in Bloomington, Indiana. He put in a good word for me, and they agreed to accept me if I maintained a B average during my senior year of high school. I did not get the grades and did not get in. My only other application was to Penn State University, where many of the kids I knew were going and where I knew I would get accepted: The path of least resistance.

I also felt a change of scenery and a new group of people would provide me the opportunity to redeem my self-image. Freedom would make me whole again. I could re-invent myself, become the sort of superstar I always dreamed of being, once I got away from the humiliations of the past. Away from abuse, away from bullies. If only it had been that simple.

# CHAPTER 3:
## *Eating Disorder U.*

*Binging, purging and running in the Marine Corps Marathon.*

*M*y first eating disorder was anorexia.
Summer, 1979. My father took me for a visit to Behrend College, a branch campus of Penn State, outside of Erie, Pennsylvania. I'd be starting out at Behrend because my high-school grades weren't good enough to allow me to go directly to Penn State's main campus. As my dad and I were walking up to the registration building, we passed two college girls. One of them looked at me and smiled, and I smiled back. After she passed us, I heard her say to her friend, "Geez, that's what's coming here for the new semester?"

Ouch. I felt, once again, like that thirteen-year-old boy who'd just been pantsed. It was a feeling I seemed to experience over and over again. Nothing is going to change unless I take control of my life, I thought. I had to take control of my weight.

My dad and I returned home, and I immediately began to deny myself food. In my mind, I was simply "dieting." And, at first, it really was just dieting. Cutting out the Chef Boyardee. Heading up to the high-school track and walking for a few miles in the early morning cloak of darkness. These were healthy impulses. As the summer went on, I continued to increase my exercise and even began to jog a little. At the same time, I kept decreasing my food intake. The weight started to come off. Soon, I was down from 260 pounds to 250. I had total control! Something I had never experienced. The power over my body was intoxicating.

One day, I was just finishing a run/walk around the neighborhood and had taken off my shirt to cool down. I heard a voice call out from a neighbor's house, "Looking good, Brian!" It was the beautiful, blond older sister of a kid I went to school with. She was sunbathing in their backyard. I turned, flushed, and managed a hoarse "thank you" that she probably did not hear. I immediately put my shirt back on. Even in the midst of a compliment, the thought that someone could see my stomach was shaming. Taking off my shirt? What was I thinking! Never again! She couldn't have been serious, I thought. I still had so much work to do.

By half-starving myself and exercising more, I dropped about thirty pounds by the time I entered Penn State Behrend. I was still not satisfied. I did not see a normal 230-pound guy in the mirror. I saw a fat, ugly teenager. Someone that pretty co-eds didn't want on their campus. A figure that didn't deserve love or to be around others. This was body dysmorphia— dramatically exaggerating or even imagining physical flaws and allowing that fantasy to shape nearly all of my interactions with the world. Starting fresh at college only seemed to exacerbate the problem—now, more than ever, I was convinced that I could finally find acceptance, but only if I could radically transform the monster I saw staring back at me every time I passed a mirror or a store-window reflection.

•

The Penn State Behrend campus is located in Wesleyville, Pennsylvania, a small town of about 3,500 people. At the time I attended, if you wanted to get groceries or to eat at a restaurant, you needed transportation. I had a beat-up Ford Granada that my dad had bought me, but I couldn't trust it to get me very far from campus. I was driving around one day not long after I arrived at school, and the Granada's hood broke off, flew up over the car, and dropped in the street behind me. I could get the thing to start only sporadically—and rarely when the weather got cold—so, for the most part, I was on foot. If I didn't eat on campus at designated times, I didn't eat. If I missed a meal and had no transportation into town, I was left with the candy and soft-drink machines for nourishment. The arrangement was fine with me. I would soon shift into full starvation mode.

That first day, I was relaxing in my dorm room, after getting it set up just the way I wanted it. I watched out my window as other new students moved boxes from cars to dorms, chatted, and said their goodbyes to proud parents. My favorite Billy Joel album, *The Stranger*, was playing softly in the background on my brand new Pioneer receiver and turntable. A pretty girl with red curly hair was hanging out right outside my dorm room window, talking to her friends in the parking lot. Our eyes met through the open window of my dorm room. I smiled. She giggled, tapped one of her friends on the shoulder, pointed at me, and said (in what sounded like a thunderous sonic boom likely heard throughout campus), "HE'S UGLY!" She repeated it again, laughing. "UGLY! UGLY!" I was devastated. She's repulsed by my weight, I thought. That old familiar feeling. I shut the window, closed the curtain, and slunk over to my bed. Humiliated. I cried myself quietly to sleep that night—a familiar ritual. Like the child sitting outside of the campfire circle at Emma Kaufmann Camp, I wanted to go home.

The next day, I woke up with a plan. I would escalate my "dieting" through sheer force of will and

reach a weight that would make me attractive, popular, and someone that women wouldn't reject on first
sight. I would never hear the word "ugly again." A familiar mantra, but, this time, I was resolved. I was a
college student—an independent adult—and it was
time to finish transforming myself.

My plan was to eat only one meal a day, at din-
nertime. My standard dinner was a small salad with
red-vinegar dressing (no oil), and a zero-calorie TAB.
I would skip breakfast and lunch and just drink water
or TAB, and occasionally down a pack of M&M's from
the candy machines to quell hunger pangs. My food
intake was less than 600 calories a day. I thought my
new diet meant I was taking charge of my problems,
but, in reality, I was losing control to an eating disorder.

I did not have either the maturity or information
to realize the strain I was putting on my body. Rapid
weight loss associated with self-starvation can have
devastating effects on a number of internal systems.
Refusing yourself food can lead to damage to every
organ. I convinced myself that what I was doing was
healthy, and, really, I didn't have good reason to think
otherwise.

In the late seventies, anorexia and other eating
disorders were rarely discussed in the media. Only
a few years after I started my dangerous diet, pop
star Karen Carpenter died of heart failure related to
anorexia. Her death began a national conversation

about eating disorders. But, in many ways, it also helped establish stereotypes about the disorder: anorexia was a disease suffered exclusively by young women—melancholic beauties who slipped away tragically, pound by pound. I never would have connected what I was doing to that stereotype. After all, I didn't want to slip away from the world, I wanted to join it. I wasn't passively letting my body deteriorate, I was willing it to be better and stronger than ever before. At least, that's what I told myself.

In fact, it is not only young women who suffer from what is clinically called anorexia nervosa. Old or young, rich or poor, male or female—anorexia touches every conceivable demographic. For me, anorexia was the self-restriction of food intake to the point of self-harm in response to a distorted self-image. Sounds a lot like the definition of body dysmorphia, and, indeed, the two disorders often go hand in hand. Body dysmorphia, however, can be characterized by a wider range of self-perceived physical flaws (not just weight) and is more often associated with a broader range of obsessive-compulsive behaviors and rituals. For those who may think they or a loved one suffers from anorexia, BDD, or both, it's important to get a proper diagnosis, because treatment may differ for each disorder.

When I began engaging in anorexic behavior, I wasn't trying to become some rail-thin model. I wanted to be a fit, attractive man. I equated acceptance with body image as I saw the good-looking, in-shape kids accepted in school. Along with my TAB diet, I also continued the exercise routine I had started over the summer. I would walk or jog late at night, when no one could see me. Slowly, I began to feel more athletic, more like I was in control of my body and less like my body was in control of me. I began obsessively weighing myself at the campus infirmary, sometimes twice a day. The more weight that came off, the more I came to think that I was in charge. I had never felt so empowered.

In that first semester of college, I was developing a full-blown eating disorder. As I became more obsessed about my appearance, I was also becoming hyper-observant and critical of shortcomings in others, as I would constantly compare perceived defects in acquaintances and rate myself against them to feel better about myself. In this way, I became what I had despised—I became a bully. My victim was one of my dorm roommates.

I shared my freshman dorm with three guys. Two of them made it abundantly clear that I was not worthy of sharing their dorm space. The fourth guy was also overweight and shy, and the two alpha males wanted him out as well. This fourth roommate was known to us as "Hawaiian Dan." Dan was from San Diego, and he always wore brightly colored Hawaiian shirts. The two "cool" guys requested that Hawaiian Dan and I switch rooms with two other buddies of theirs, but we refused. I was crushed that these out-going, good-looking kids wanted to boot me out. I was surprised that my recent sense of empowerment over my weight wasn't already translating into popularity. Somehow, I needed to make it clear that I belonged with them—not with shy, chubby outcasts.

Soon, I began a relentless campaign of bullying against Dan. I would leave letters on Dan's bunk telling him what a loser he was and asking him to move out, conveniently ignoring the fact that the two dorm-room alphas regarded me as part of the same reject brigade and wanted me to move out as well. I called Dan "fat." I called him a "pig." I told him I didn't want him around. Of course, no matter how much I bullied Dan, it was not going to make me feel better about myself or help me gain acceptance among the thin, muscular, attractive kids. I was merely repeating the cycle of harmful verbal abuse that I had experienced at home, at school, and on the playground. It did nothing for me, but it felt good in the moment: Like my crash diet, it helped me feel like I was in control. The lesson I learned far too late is that, with body dysmorphia, the behaviors that made me feel most in control were often the most destructive for myself and others. Eventually, Dan's brother, a much bigger guy than I was, came up to the school and confronted me, threatening to beat the hell out of me if I continued to bully his brother. That's how bad I had made things for Dan. The confrontation was a wake-up call, and I left Dan alone after that, but I never made things right with him.

Soon, I'd transfer to the main campus of Penn State and would never see Dan again. Being a bully did not make me feel better about myself, and being confronted about my bullying didn't lead to any epiphanies about my destructive behavior—or fix the reflection in the mirror.

•

Part of the way through my freshman year, I realized self-starvation was not enough. Even with the most focused of minds, I couldn't sustain a diet of lettuce, TAB, and M&M's for the long term. It left me feeling too weak and distracted. In my mind, it also wasn't working. I still saw the same fat kid in the mirror. This realization, however, did not lead me to start eating well. It only meant that I had to find new tactics to achieve my goal.

I knew there was a small group of kids like me who had at least semi-operational transportation. I got into that group. On the weekends, we would go into town and go bowling. We'd then hit either the Perkins Pancake House or a local buffet. My new plan was to starve myself during the week and gorge myself on weekends. Those stacks of pancakes and two-hour binges at the endless buffet added up to a lot of calories, but food binging also brought back familiar feelings of relief—this was how I had comforted my-self as a child. After the comfort came the guilt and depression.

Then, for the first time, I began purging my food.

I did not know that this was called bulimia. I simply knew that, by throwing up after meals, I could have my pancakes and not eat them, too. The actual act of vomiting, combined with the knowledge that I was maintaining control over my body, gave me an incredible emotional-tension release like I had never before experienced. I can compare it only to the high I would get later in life from doing a line of cocaine. However, much like cocaine, after I purged, the de-pression would return even more intensely because I was ashamed of what I had done. It was a vicious cycle of self-destruction.

Every time we pigged out at one of these plac-es, I would get home as quickly as possible, turn up the music in my dorm, turn on the faucet in the bathroom, and then jam my fingers down my throat. Sometimes it became quite a covert operation to ac-complish this without my roommates catching on. Many times I claimed I was sick or that I'd too much to drink. That was usually enough. When you're eigh-teen years old in a college town, seeing a roommate puke simply does not set off any alarms. And, even if my roommates had thought something was odd, no one, at that time, would ever suspect a young man might have a dangerous eating disorder.

I empathize with any young man being too ashamed and embarrassed to seek treatment for bulimia or anorexia. Even today, there isn't much of a national conversation about men and eating disorders, and there's even less dialogue concerning men and BDD. Even in my early treatment for depression, I wouldn't admit to any harmful behavior related to eating. I talked about failed relationships or parental discord. Anything but binging and purging or shame about my body. My reluctance was probably not uncommon. Many of those who suffer from the disease tell no one. Some die.

The stigma for men talking about their eating disorders is reinforced by the lack of any public voice discussing the problem. There is no doubt that, in the Internet-driven, hot-bod image explosion of the *GQ* generation, men have become more aggressive in trying to emulate the perfect males they see in the media. As of the writing of this book, there simply aren't many iconic male celebrities or other public figures who have discussed struggles with body-image disorders. Perhaps when more come forward, young men will be better able to contextualize their problems. When I was eighteen, I simply had no vocabulary for telling others about my behavior. And even if I had, I don't know if I would have used it. Also, I believed that what I was doing was temporary—once I was thin enough to have reached my goal, all my social problems would be solved, and I'd have a normal diet again. I would have the happy life and popularity I thought I saw others enjoying. Unfortunately, the mirror always told me there was a problem with my appearance.

Whatever the initial motivation, eating disorders can take on a momentum of their own once they begin. Between the isolating shame, the comforting rituals of self-mastery, and physiological quirks of bodies in starvation mode, anorexic and bulimic behaviors can become habits with the strength of full-blown addiction.

•

Fall, 1980. I was excited to transfer from my small branch campus near Erie to the Penn State main campus in University Park, Pennsylvania. It's a beautiful campus of over forty thousand students in central Pennsylvania—so idyllic and isolated from the world that it is dubbed "Happy Valley." There were tons of people, an atmosphere of belonging to something big and fun, and students of all shapes and sizes from around the world. By the time I arrived on campus, I felt I had taken control of my body. I was running every day, and I was getting thinner and thinner. I was still starving myself. I was still binging and purging. Shower, sink faucets, and flushing toilets in the communal dorm bathrooms hid the sounds I needed to disguise from my new dorm mates. Every time I purged, I thought, This should do it! Now I'm ready to be accepted and popular! I was even rooming with an old high-school friend. I can't fail!

Unfortunately, my hope was all based on a faulty premise. Simply getting thin was not enough to fix the shattered image. And my distorted sense of self couldn't be fixed simply by fleeing from my problems. You can't escape your past, and you can't escape your genetic destiny. The only way to fix the image is to confront the past, deal with the destructive behaviors, and accept yourself for who you are, quirks and all.

I lived on the same dorm floor as a bunch of red-shirt football players. Everyone mingled, had parties and hung out. Everyone was having a lot of fun. But not me. I couldn't get it going, and I couldn't figure out why. Some part of me felt like I was still just that ugly outsider kid standing up against the bleachers at the high-school dance. I was still unnerved by all those derisive words I'd heard over the years, even if I wasn't hearing them now. Getting thin through starvation had not changed anything. Taking control of my weight was not enough. I felt I still had to fix— something.

But fix what? I had become a skinny guy. But in my mind, I still had love handles. I was still aware of my stomach fat— I could practically see fat cells and measure their presence with laser precision. I had to try harder! I kept restricting my food, purging, and running increasingly long distances every day to force the weight off.

At night, I'd have a persistent gut ache, not just from my extreme eating behaviors, but from pure, intense loneliness and isolation in a dorm full of potential friends. I thought they didn't want me to be part of it all, but, in reality, I was afraid to be a part of the fun. I was afraid to risk being told I wasn't wanted. Better to not even try. Better to run alone. And run I did. I was the Forrest Gump of my dormitory floor. If you did not see me, I was running. I missed class to run. I would run ten miles in the morning and ten miles in the evening, six or even seven days a week. Weather was not an obstacle: I would run in sub-zero temperatures, blizzards, or pouring rain. After the run came Domino's Pizza, and maybe a two-pound bag of peanut M&M's. Those were the staples of my binge-and-purge routine. Then to bed. And in the morning, time for another run.

No one cared. This was college. Drunk kids—and maybe even others with eating disorders—were puking. I saw it. I heard it. At least in that way, I fit right in.

October, 1981. A beautiful, cool, crisp, Saturday afternoon. The Penn State Nittany Lions were playing a home game against the Boston College Eagles. There would be close to eighty-five thousand people in Beaver Stadium. Penn State was having a great football year. It seemed like everyone in the dorm went. I couldn't imagine going. I loved Nittany Lion football, but I hated that feeling I got in the pit of my stomach when I felt like an outsider in a big crowd. I yearned to be a part of that cheering camaraderie of Nittany Lion fans all geared out in blue and white. But what's the point? Being alone is easier; alone, you know no rejection. I ran with alone. I ran.

It was an easy choice that day. Perfect weather to do the impossible. My plan was to run from University Park to Altoona, Pennsylvania. Was I nuts? Altoona was forty-three miles away! That's eighty-six miles round-trip. I was not an ultra-endurance runner. I was, however, mentally ill. There was a rational part of my mind quietly telling me it was impossible. I also knew that, whatever happened, by the time I got back, the football game would be over.

It was late morning, about 10 or 11 A.M. Students and alumni were already on their way to Beaver Stadium for pre-game tailgating. The kids on my dorm floor were excited, making banners, and happily chattering as they always did on game Saturdays. I did not want to see them, hear them, or feel their presence. I wanted the orderly, predictable, linear silence of footfalls on the pavement. I put twenty dollars and two NoDoz caffeine pills in my pocket, and I started my run. The caffeine pills gave me an extra kick when I got tired. I gave no thought to how I would get home when I inevitably tired, cramped up (I hadn't even brought water), or just mentally quit.

I got about seventeen miles out and could run

no farther. I was surrounded in all directions by the
rolling farmland of central Pennsylvania: A beautiful
landscape for solitude. The silly reality of my endeav-
or hit me. I wasn't going to make it. Not even close.
I didn't care. It wasn't about achievement. It was
about finding sanity in doing the insane. By the time
I ran-walked-ran the seventeen miles back, the game
would be over. It was dark when I got back to University Park. I walked through town. Students were still
celebrating Penn State's 38-7 win. I went to Domino's
and bought a pizza. I ate it in my dorm room with my
old familiar friend, bulimia. Then down the hallway
to the toilet.

Life became a routine of running, binging, and
purging. Classes were an afterthought, but I actually
did okay in the classroom. I chose a relatively easy
major, and I had good short-term memory. I also had
the discipline of a long-distance runner, an obsessive-
compulsive mindset, and no social life to distract me.
It was almost like my binging and purging routine.
Study all night and vomit the information back out
onto a piece of paper the next day. But the classroom
offered no sense of personal accomplishment. My life
revolved around finding those rare moments when I
felt good about my appearance.

When I had to take a day off from running, I might
head downstairs to play the piano in the dorm community area. "Scenes From an Italian Restaurant" by
Billy Joel, or my new standard at the time, "Babe" by

Styx. I hoped a pretty girl would notice and say hello. Someone who would help me fight through it all and become a normal, loved, and loving person.

Late fall semester, 1981. My first college crush! I met Joanne in criminology class. Tall and slender, with curly dark hair. I made sure we always sat next to each other. We laughed and made small talk. That was the best I could do.

Joanne's family lived not far from my home in Pittsburgh. At Penn State, she was in Simmons Hall, the dorm directly across from mine. Maybe I could accidently bump into her in the Simmons cafeteria? But I was terrified of walking into the cafeteria, of eating alone. With happy people staring at me, wondering about my loneliness. Whispering about me, the loser eating by himself. I'd never have the confidence to ask out Joanne. I didn't know how—I still had the social skills of a child.

And like a school boy pulling a girl's hair in class, I resorted to a childish prank to get her attention. I called her up one day and pretended I was a DJ from a local radio station. I told her that if she made it from her dorm to the pizza parlor in five minutes, she would get a free pie. My friends and I laughed as we watched her and a friend bolt out of the door for a pizza that never was. I was a jerk. But I was a jerk that people were laughing with instead of at. Acceptance!

Then the guilt. The next day, in class, Joanne told me that some "asshole" had sent her on a phony

pizza run. I hated myself and felt my body temperature rise as I tried to admit what I had done. The
words never came out. I had done to her what I had
done to Hawaiian Dan during my freshman year. I had
been ugly to her to feel better about my ugliness. I
ordered a pizza that night. I was going to take it over
to her dorm and confess. I called her but could find
no words. I hung up. I felt frozen. I ate that pizza and
then purged it. The release of shame and guilt with
each retch was liberating. Another night down. Keep
moving forward. One step after another.

At the end of my sophomore year, I had not giv-
en up on Joanne, despite never having the nerve to
engage in anything but classroom small-talk. But now
it was summer. How to meet her while school was
out? I had a plan! I would impress her with what I did
best. I would run.

That summer, back at home, I would run from
my parents' house to Upper St. Clair, Pennsylvania,
where she lived with her parents—about seventeen
miles round trip. I would run by her house over and
over. I would wait for her to come out. We would
make small talk. We would live happily ever after.
What I was doing was practically stalking, but it was
the only way I knew how to communicate. I can't say
how many times I ran circles through her neighborhood and past her house. If only she'd come out of
that damn house, I'd think. She never did.

I actually became a pretty good runner and

ended up competing in races, including nine marathons. I finished eight of them. But the reason I ran was not to better myself athletically. It was because long-distance running fit my introverted nature and helped me control my body. It helped me escape the loneliness of crowded rooms, crowded stadiums, crowded bars. The loneliness of the road was preferable. Solitary, compulsive behavior was a drug that I embraced like I would later embrace alcohol and cocaine. It didn't matter. I still saw exaggerated flaws and imperfections. The solution was to run more and purge more. And then, as my college years came and went, I would start to drink more.

•

January 1, 1983. The Penn State Nittany Lions were playing the Georgia Bulldogs for the NCAA Division One college football national championship in New Orleans, Louisiana. It was winter break. Most of my friends had gone home or to the game. Those left in town gathered at the local bars to watch. I got drunk by myself in my dorm, hoping that it would give me the courage to walk into one of these bars and join the party. I remember the feeling of emptiness as I walked the back alley just off College Avenue, where some of the bars were located. I longed to be a part of it. Instead I was a college drunk, creeping the alley.

I walked into a bar called the Shandygaff. It was

packed with people cheering for Penn State. Everyone was having a good time. Everyone seemed to have a group of friends. But why would they allow me to join them? I went to the local McDonald's and binged on Quarter Pounders. I went back to my dorm and purged. For years afterward, if the subject came up, I would claim that I had actually been at the game. A meaningless lie, but one that prevented me from reliving the self-loathing I felt when the game was mentioned.

The night also represents part of a larger a transition—I was getting close to graduating college, and, at the same time, I was graduating from one set of destructive behaviors to another. I was continuing to binge, purge, and exercise excessively, but I was replacing dieting with drinking. I would often get drunk alone before heading out to the bars by myself, hoping the buzz would make me feel good enough to be socially outgoing. It never worked. At the bar, I'd simply drink alone some more. I would be so ashamed when I got home that I would stuff myself with the familiar pizza, a two-pound bag of peanut M&M's, or fast food, and then purge it all.

I also started experimenting with diuretics and laxatives during that time. During my senior year, Ex-lax became a standard supplement to bulimic behavior. I remember when I added that to my BDD arsenal. I had just come off the bus from Pittsburgh to Penn State after visiting my parents. I had been limiting my caloric intake severely for a couple days while running long distances. I got off the bus and immediately headed for McDonald's and binged. The guilt was overwhelming. My pants felt tight. I was in a panic. I decided that, in addition to binging at my apartment (I was no longer in the dorms), I would throw a few bars of the chocolate Ex-lax into the mix. Soon, between the lack of calories, extreme exercise routines, and dehydration from purging and laxatives, I was in a constant state of malnutrition and dehydration. Despite being apparently fit, I was sometimes too weak to get out of bed.

By the end of my time at Penn State, I had accumulated an impressive set of destructive behaviors. I lashed out at those who could most help or understand me, becoming a bully whenever I felt the proximity of real intimacy.

The link between all these symptoms is that they are obsessive. To an outside observer, these behaviors may seem self-obsessive. As I tell my stories, my readers might think, "Brian doesn't have a disease, he's just vain and narcissistic." It may seem like there's no difference between this psychological disorder and simply being a self-absorbed douchebag. Women suffering from BDD are often seen as stuck up. It's a big reason many BDD sufferers do not want to talk about their issues—they don't want to admit to being so self-absorbed. Even close friends and family may believe that their loved ones are simply

acting in a vain manner, seeking superficial reassurance. Like many sufferers of BDD, when I received the
reassurance I asked for, I felt I was being placated.

It's important to be open about your feelings
and seek help if you think you or anyone you love
is experiencing symptoms of BDD. Oftentimes, the
disorder is simply too easy to dismiss as the sharp
edges of a difficult personality. And the fear of open,
honest dialogue is even greater when eating disorders are involved.

Eating disorders have been a core feature of my
experience with body dysmorphia and one of the
most difficult aspects of BDD for me to talk about. As
I went through severe emotional battles within myself for decades over food intake, I never opened up
to anyone close to me. It took me years to broach the
subject—even after I started counseling. I came up
with multitudes of reasons to stay silent with psychiatric professionals in the most protected of settings. I
told myself that only women obsess about their bodies. If I talked about it, I thought, I'd also be question-
ing my masculinity.

While I have not engaged in binging and purging
behavior since 2006, whenever I eat too much, the
thought that I can get relief by sticking my fingers
down my throat will invariably go through my head.
I still get a feeling of calmness and relief at just the
thought of doing it. I have learned not to succumb
to such thoughts and feelings. As with many BDD be-

haviors, the urge never really goes away—my healing has come through self-awareness and the resolve to replace those self-destructive thoughts with positive ones.

# CHAPTER 4:
## *Drunk, Drugged, and Delirious*

*The eyes always tell the story.*

*A*ccording to organizations such as the National Institute of Health, body dysmorphia and substance abuse often go hand in hand. Some studies suggest that as many as half of all BDD sufferers have some history of substance abuse, and as many as one third of all BDD sufferers have a dependence on alcohol. As with eating disorders, substance-abuse disorders are often extreme attempts to compensate for depression, feelings of isolation, and distorted self-perception or low self-esteem. So many of the truly damaging symptoms of BDD are radical, self-destructive efforts to transform the self. Even though drugs and alcohol can cause severe physical and mental harm, they offered me an easy path to feeling like that new person I wanted to see in the mirror. They offered a convenient lie.

While I had experimented with marijuana and alcohol in high school, it was more about wanting acceptance than creating a different self-image. Marijuana never made me feel better about myself; it made me indifferent to my appearance, which was better than nothing. Now, I wanted to reshape how others saw me. If I was fat and ugly but also fun enough to be included, that was fine with me. If I was part of the crowd while getting hammered, well then, at least I was part of the crowd. During college, I would have loved to be part of the crowd getting drunk at football games and fraternity keggers, but I had no idea how to break through my self-imposed isolation.

The few frat parties I went to had familiar results: I was an outsider in a crowd of kids getting drunk and having fun. In my mind, everyone was laughing at me and wondering what I was doing there. In the movie *Animal House*, there is a scene at a party with a group of outcasts—blind, fat, ugly, and disabled—sitting on a couch. The unwanted. I was one of those outcasts, doing the exact same thing. Sitting on the frat couch with my beer, getting hammered, talking to no one. Not being talked to by anyone, radiating negativity, convinced pass-ersby were judging me. Alcohol sometimes made me feel a bit more open to talking to strangers, but even buzzed, I had too much anxiety to open my mouth. The thoughts would not travel to my tongue. It made me miserable.

After a couple of frat parties, I gave up on being part of the drinking crowd. It was so much better being alone and creating a fiction in my mind of what it would be like when things changed for me. My mind and its ability to create vivid, movie-like fantasies of a different life was my only tool for experiencing the feelings of social acceptance. I would dream that a better life would be mine when I lost a few more pounds. When I lost those love handles. Once I had my body in the shape I wanted—and with a little liquid courage—I was sure I'd be admired by all.

As I moved stolidly through my senior year, trying to kill each day of loneliness with long runs, alcohol, and extreme eating behaviors, I still had to figure out what I wanted to do with my life. I originally wanted to be a police officer. I applied for several jobs in different cities, but I couldn't score high enough on the tests. I didn't care enough. I remember sitting in the testing room of the Mt. Lebanon Police Department daydreaming about going on a long run that afternoon, while the proctor gave instructions for the exam. I didn't hear a word he said.

Staying a student seemed the best course. I

knew what worked as a student. I had a couple buddies who were taking the LSAT, the law school admission test. What the hell. No effort to walk in there and take it. Didn't study. Walked in and took it cold. To my great surprise, I did okay. So, law school it was. I could not have cared less about the legal profession or any kind of social justice. I just wanted to survive day to day, year to year. Another few years of school could put off any long-term decisions about my future.

During the summer after graduating college, I ratcheted up my running. I moved back home and took a job as store detective at Joseph Horne's Department stores in downtown Pittsburgh. I spent my days trying to catch shoplifters by sneaking around and hiding behind two-way mirrors. The store in downtown Pittsburgh was close to ten miles from my parents' home. Every morning, I would wake up at 6 AM, put on my backpack with a change of clothes, and run to work. I would change into my work clothes at the downtown YMCA. I would take the bus home. By the time fall came and I started law school, my weight had dropped to just under 170 pounds—down more than 80 pounds from my top weight in high school. At 170, my mind saw the exact same thing in the mirror as at 250. I had to try harder.

I started that fall at the University of Pittsburgh School of Law. Once again, a whole new chance to remake myself. Of course, I brought my baggage with me to law school. I continued binging and purging into my first year, and I was still running obsessively as well. My bulimic behavior shifted toward drinking and binge eating when I went out to the bars. My typical routine was to buy the cheapest tequila, drink most of the bottle before I left my apartment, and hit the bars alone. I almost never achieved the result I was looking for. Drinking did not make me more outgoing, more attractive, or more self-confident. It often made me an introverted drunk and my depression even worse. As in college, these drunken nights invariably ended up with me adding a food binge to the mix. Often it involved heading over to the White Tower burger joint not far from campus and inhaling about a dozen burgers, most eaten within ten minutes on the way home, and purging when I got back to my place. Or maybe purging in some dark alley of Oakland, where the Pitt campus was located, if my roommates were home and I did not want to be discovered.

Fall, 1983. I've just moved in with a fellow student. He's smart, driven, and knows people. I know no one, but I want to get to know people. I need to change my outlook. Students are already forming cliques and study groups. I'm on the outside once more. These are future lawyers with ambition and focus—qualities I don't possess. What to do?

I walk into a liquor store. A pint of Jose Cuervo. On to the Giant Eagle grocery store. A liter of TAB. Within an hour, both are empty. I am shit-faced, alone in my apartment. Then off to Calico's, the law school hangout. Brian sits at the bar. Drunk Brian gets drunker. It's not working—I'm not feeling cool yet. Mind-bending depression sets in. This sucks! I hate law school! Off to Roy Rogers across the street. Unlimited salad bar to help soak up the alcohol.

Time to get home. Where the hell am I? Suddenly, I find myself outside the old Forbes Field, where the Pittsburgh Pirates once played. Where my hero, Robert Clemente once roamed right field. The isolated center-field wall, still standing as a historic monument, is as good as place as any. A good, stomach-emptying purge right about where Bill Mazeroski hit his game-winning home run in the 1960 World Series. That familiar release of everything I hate about myself. That familiar high. I think of those days collecting baseball cards, sitting with dad in the sun, Clemente on the field.

The world is spinning. I hope I can find my way home.

One night, while stumbling home across the Pitt campus, I ran across an Alcoholics Anonymous pamphlet in the White Tower. The sort designed for students exactly like me to read. "Are You an Alcoholic?" its title bluntly asked. I gave that question, and others inside the pamphlet, some serious thought.

"Have you ever missed work or school because of your drinking?"—Yes, but that's okay, because I can still run with a hangover.

"Have you had problems with drinking the past year?" —What kind of problems? I'm a college student. We all get stinking drunk and puke up our meals.

"Do you have blackouts?" —Is passing out a blackout?

"Have you ever sought help?" —Listen. I am clearly NOT an alcoholic! Alcoholism is for smelly, unshaven bums living under a bridge. I'm not an alcoholic. Putting that behind me. Going to purge up my White Tower burgers before I pass out. I'm not an alcoholic, I'm a normal student. I'm going to be a lawyer.

Of course, that remained to be seen. My late-night drinking cycles were not yet threatening my law "career," but I wasn't impressing professors with my grades, either. I made no bones about the fact that my multi-hour runs were more important to me than class. I did only what I needed to get by.

•

Fall, 1984. Emily was twenty-six, almost three years older than me. We were both boarders at a house close to the law school. She was a graduate of

Brandeis and was working on her graduate degree. She was thin and pretty with short brown hair, and she was very outgoing. I also admired her ability to keep to herself—as socially confident as she was, she didn't feel the desire to hit the bar scene or join every party. I think Emily viewed me as a "project"—someone shy and withdrawn who she could help draw out into the world, while at the same time locating some confidence in me to help me be myself. At first, we were just friends.

I ended up losing my virginity to Emily on a blanket in the basement of the boarding house. I was drunk, of course. Alcohol took away some of my self-loathing and fear of intimacy in that moment.

I was inexperienced. I had no concept of what sex should be like and was ashamed of my body. I was afraid to look at her, because that meant she would be looking at me. Our eyes never met the entire time. I did not find the sex itself shameful, but I felt mortified at being exposed as an inexperienced child. She had to know it was my first time. Twenty-three years old! What guy waits that long! What should have been something I remembered with fondness instead became something that made me ill to think about. Women want men, not children.

But somehow, as uncomfortable as I was with Emily, I didn't spoil things entirely. One night after our basement encounter, while we were watching television together, she casually suggested that we have dinner sometime. A real date. She must have known I'd never initiate anything on my own. She was right. I would have never said a word.

September 16, 1984. My first romantic date EVER! Prior to the basement with Emily, I had never kissed a girl. What do people do on dates? Dinner means I could get drunk. Conversation might be easier with alcohol. Still, I could not imagine being comfortable just sitting across from a date all night, being studied. I'd have to come up with something else besides a romantic dinner.

I didn't know much about soul music, but I had recently heard for the first time George Benson's rendition of "On Broadway." I loved it, and it ran through my head constantly. I put myself in the place of George and imagined what it would be like to be driven. To be a star. To be talented at something. Memories of those childhood dreams permeated my thoughts.

*They say the women treat you fine on Broadway*
*but lookin' at them just gives me the blues*

I knew exactly what George was singing about—wanting to be part of the beautiful crowd had made me feel down for a long time. But I had more than the blues. I was clinically depressed. I had no idea what that was or meant in terms of my life. I just knew it sucked. If I could only be "on Broadway" it would all change. I had never been to New York City, but my Broadway was the mirror in my bathroom. I wanted to be able to see myself in bright lights—or at least flattering lighting. Now, I had a woman interested in me, and maybe it was time to chase my dreams again.

I had to hear George sing the song live. It would inspire me to seek more than simply to get through each day. The song would be my anthem. With George in my corner and Emily by my side, I would make a fresh start, and, this time, it would last.

Not long after we agreed to go out on a real date, I saw it in the paper: George Benson is coming to Pittsburgh's Syria Mosque. I had my date plans set. Emily and I went to the concert together. It was a powerful, energizing performance that gave me the fresh resolve I'd hoped for. George had brought me part way to Broadway. That night, I was a man.

Emily and I started dating. I was wanted! It was a new feeling, to be desired. But, even after we'd been together a while, I never let Emily know about the extent of my problems. I couldn't even admit to myself some of the dysmorphia-inspired thoughts and feelings I was having. There was no way I was about to discuss them with a woman who seemed to be attracted to me. Still, Emily was smart enough to figure some of them out. My drinking was already serious enough that she tried to help me move past it, along with my incredible shyness and introversion.

Soon, she encouraged me to try out therapy for the first time.

At Emily's recommendation, I tried EST (often written as "est"), which stands for Erhard Seminars Training. I knew about EST already from my mother's participation. She had pitched it to me years earlier, and I had refused. I viewed it as just an extension of her screaming-in-the-closet therapy. Ironic that the first girl I ever dated was, like my mother, involved in EST. I wonder what Freud would say about that.

EST was a popular group-treatment method in the seventies and eighties, supplanting the fads of the previous decade. It found numerous celebrity adherents such as John Denver, Diana Ross, and Yoko Ono. EST combined group dialogs with healthy doses of psychoanalytic language and a splash of Zen Buddhism, all whipped together by Werner Erhard, a former encyclopedia salesman. Training seminars were held across the country and would typically take two intense weekends to complete. The goal of the seminars was to talk through self-inhibiting patterns and replace them with a mental state of enlightenment and purpose. Those who broke through to enlightenment over one of the weekends were said to have "got it."

With Emily set to participate with me, and with money given to me by my mother (who was thrilled I was going), I participated in an EST seminar in Cleveland. I remember a bunch of people sitting on the floor of a giant meeting room, listening to people tell us how to "get it."

Going in, I had no idea what I was supposed to "get," but I was becoming more self-aware of the fact that I had issues. I did not know how to define those issues in terms of specific disorders, but I knew that my behavior was becoming more and more destructive. I knew I was drinking too much. I knew that I felt alone in the most crowded of rooms. While I still did not know what bulimia was, I knew that running 15–20 miles a day and then binging and purging at night was not healthy and was intensifying my state of depression. These had become compulsive behaviors. I could not help myself. That was enough at that time to at least move me in the direction of reaching out for help.

My memories of the weekend sessions in Cleveland are hazy. They did not allow us to use the bathroom during each day-long session. I recall that some people had catheters going into bottles. The only other lessons I took from the seminar were that I should talk to strangers in elevators and give the company behind EST lots of money.

Though EST didn't work for me, one thing was clear: I was searching. Searching for that magic spell that would rid me of my demons. Perhaps for people who are relatively sound psychologically, self-help sessions such as EST can be positive experiences. Primal therapy, group meditation, or even a motivational self-help book might be all such people need to feel like they are back on track with their lives. But for those who suffer personality disorders, substance-abuse problems, or other grave psychological conditions, quick fixes through such self-help programs can do more harm then good. For instance, they can lead to greater discouragement and depression when they don't work. Sometimes, they can be traumatic. There are solutions out there, but they take time and commitment, and can't be achieved over a couple of weekends—even without bathroom breaks. BDD recovery is a long-term process that differs for everyone.

I returned to Pittsburgh relieved but lonelier than ever, searching once again for a solution to an expanding list of personal problems. Of course, in my mind, deeper problems called for even more radical solutions. And my next attempt at self-help was, indeed, radical. It was the summer of 1985. I joined the Officer Candidate program of the U.S. Marine Corps.

I did not join because I was patriotic or looking for a noble cause. I did not want to be one of a "few good men." I joined because I wanted to able to look myself in the mirror and see a man. Emily and I had broken up shortly after the EST seminar, but I still wanted to become that man she wanted to see. No more fat Brian. No more alcoholic Brian. No more shy Brian. They would all be gone. I wanted to see a

Brian who I could love and who others could love as well. The Marines could turn me into one good man. The plan I worked out with the recruiter was that I would go through Officer Candidate School (OCS); then, I would attend the Basic School in Quantico, Virginia; then after I finished law school, I would go through the JAG corps training to be a Marine lawyer.

It all sounded great to me. I would get into exceptional physical shape and gain self-confidence. The millions of shattered pieces of mirror would be miraculously put back together in ten weeks. Humpty Dumpty never fared so well.

I was also not going in alone. A law-school classmate and friend was also joining. He was very gung-ho, and his enthusiasm and excitement buoyed my confidence. If he could do it, I could. We trained together to take the required physical-fitness entrance test. When the time came to ship off to Quantico, I was feeling better about myself than I had in a long time. I was not binging and purging, and had mostly quit drinking. For a short time, I was able to focus on the positive behavior of improving my overall physical health to do well in OCS and the hope of making myself into a different person.

In reality, what I was doing was, at its core, no different than the binging and purging, anorexia, or binge drinking I had engaged in since college. I was looking for someone or something else to change me. Basic training, of course, isn't a therapist's office. The goal of basic training is not to make young men feel good about themselves. It's about breaking down the ego of the individual and replacing it with the ego of the group, so that everyone can depend on each other in hostile situations. The Marines have produced tens of thousands of brave and brilliant soldiers. I simply had the wrong mindset. As with self-help, basic training is no solution for those of us who are trying to overcome substantive psychological problems.

By my second day at Quantico I was completely overwhelmed. I went from being a loner, fueling my unhealthy obsessions at my leisure, to having to obey a platoon sergeant and sergeant instructor whose job it was to degrade me. They were trying to break me down and then build me up, but I was already broken. Soon I was confused—and terrified that I had made a huge mistake. On our second day, we all had to go in front of the platoon captain for a brief interview.

"Son, what were your scores on the PT test?"

"This officer candidate thought he did pretty well."

"Son, let me tell you something. You're pretty arrogant. You did not do well at all. You are not in very good shape. If you don't get those scores up, you won't make it here."

The captain went on about my arrogance and unworthiness to be a U.S. Marine. In doing his job, he had trashed the one remaining pillar of my self-confidence—my physical fitness. He was a grown man telling me I'd never become a grown man myself. I heard the voice of my mom. I heard the voices of everyone who had ever picked on me or made fun of my weight. It was too much. I was frightened and lost. The final nail in the coffin of my military career was the realization that they were going to shave my head. I had never thought about it before I joined. It seems superficial, but, for someone who already saw himself as a deformed man, it was terrifying. I knew right then I was not staying in the Marines.

I did not want to DOR (Discharge On Request), as that would humiliate me even more. It was made clear within the platoon and by the sergeants that DOR was a badge of shame, failure, and unworthiness. As it happened, I had been having some knee pain, as was normal for someone who was running more than eighty miles a week. Nothing out of the ordinary, and nothing that limited me. But I had a way out. Or at least some time to think. They sent me to the military hospital at Fort Belvoir, Virginia, to be examined. I knew I had "runner's knee" if anything at all. It was something I was accustomed to and could have dealt with in OCS. After some conversation, the Navy corpsman who examined me knew what the deal was. He had seen it before. He asked me a simple question. "Do you want to go home?" I gave him a simple answer. "Yes."

My time in the Marine Corps was over with a discharge. They pulled me out of the officer candidate barracks and stuck me in a "White Elephant," an old World War II-style barracks, along with all the others who had been discharged for one reason or another. They might as well have painted a big "L" for "Loser" on the side of the building. I could not look any of the other rejects in the eye. I would see myself. A loser. A relieved loser, but a loser nonetheless.

I have often regretted not sticking it out, and I've wondered what my life would be like if I had. I also know that, at that time, it was not something I could have gone through. Body dysmorphia did not fit with the Marine lifestyle. It wasn't just the calculated abuse. I was scared of changes as small as getting my head shaved. I became "thought fixated" on the fact that having no hair would make me a reject. No one would ever want me again. I had to get out of there before that happened! I managed to escape before I ever saw the razor. In the end, I was simply looking for someone to fix me. Not even the Marines could do that—only I could.

•

Ultimately, I coasted through law school with no idea of what I would do upon graduation. All I cared about was running and getting drunk when I had the money. But three years of school had done what I wanted them to. They allowed me to continue to avoid facing my future. I cared as much about law when I left as I did when I entered: Not at all. I still didn't know what I wanted to do with my life, but I did know where I wanted to be, and it wasn't Pittsburgh. I had returned to my hometown only because Pitt Law was the best school to accept me. I came out of school as I went in—alone. I had developed no bonds in law school. I had no friends from college or high school that I had stayed in close touch with. The feeling of loneliness in a city where I had lived my whole life was unbearable. I needed a fresh start. Like Steve Austin, the Bionic Man, I needed to rebuild myself—bigger, stronger, faster.

Time to get the hell out of Dodge. Dallas, here I come! It seemed perfect for me. Both of my brothers lived there. In their company, everything would be different. I would be fortified by the bond of brothers, which our father had emphasized from our youth. Never leave them. Never abandon them. They could save me with their love and companionship, even if I had no interest in saving myself.

Little did I realize that Dallas would be a springboard for taking my destructive behavior to a new level. I would discover something that made me feel like a winner. A new person. A handsome guy. A *GQ* model. For short bursts, it would completely fix what I saw in the mirror; it would also lead to the lowest moments of my life.

I had been to Dallas a couple of times to see my brothers. I loved those visits. Young, pretty women were everywhere. My older brother Mark was a popular man about town, and he took me to several nightclubs. The first time a woman asked me to dance was at a club in Dallas. We were at a popular nightspot called Fast and Cool. She was tall, thin, blue-eyed, and pretty in a Daryl Hannah sort of way, but with the classic Dallas big hair that was popular at the time. As she walked toward me, I started to sweat in the short-sleeved, blue-striped shirt that my brother had lent me. Memories sprang up of that Sadie Hawkins high-school dance so many years earlier. The pretty woman told me she loved my shirt and asked me to dance. We danced once. I never knew her name. I never saw her again. The feeling of being asked to dance by a total stranger, years before I had my first kiss with Emily, was so strong and empowering that I began to associate Dallas with romance. I wanted to feel like that all the time. It had to be the shirt. It had to be the place. I knew where I wanted to be.

Labor Day, 1986. When I arrived in Dallas, my brothers were there for me. Mark picked me up at the bus station. I would live with him until I found a job. He, of course, had his own circle of friends, as did Jeff. Not long after arriving, I went to work for the City of Dallas in their office of property management, buying rights of way for public-works projects. I hated it! It was boring, but it was a paycheck. Though my job was dull, I made great friends who would introduce me to the party scene. Soon I felt slightly less alone, less isolated.

Dallas was a yuppie's paradise. At that time, the city was just coming out of an economic boom and was a very young town. People loved to party. The bars were packed every night, and I had my trusty striped shirt that had worked its magic once before. I dove right in.

The thing I loved most about Dallas was that its nightlife had more women than I had ever seen in my life. At that time, it was considered one of the best places in the country for guys because of the girl/guy ratio favoring men. I even moved into the area that was known as the biggest singles complex in the world at the time, "the Village." Living in the Village made me crazy. I even added a dangling earring to my arsenal when I went out. I tried anything to get women to come up and talk to me. Between the aggressiveness of Dallas women, the blue striped shirt, the earring, and a bottle of tequila before I went out, I couldn't miss. That became the pattern. A familiar one. A bottle of booze stuck in my cowboy boots, drunk in a corner in a bar, waiting to be talked to. I added one more tactic. I would constantly yawn. Seem strange? It worked. Eventually some young woman would see that as her opening and come up and ask me if I was tired. The opening I needed. When drunk, once I got past the fear of being told I was fat and ugly, I would carry on a conversation.

Out with my friends, chasing women, I could be happy. And I was healthier when I first moved to Dallas. But when I was home alone in my apartment, the pain of who I really was could sometimes become intolerable. Intense loneliness. Wanting something out of life but having no idea what it was. Afraid to look at myself in the mirror. It was in Dallas, obsessed more than ever with my appearance and fitting in, that I first remember my BDD tics taking the forms that that would follow me through adulthood. The full-body inspection of my fat in the shower. The compulsive checking of my increasingly receding hairline. Staring at myself naked for inordinate amounts of time in the bathroom mirror every morning. Measuring my love handles with my eyes. It was beginning.

I needed more powerful medicine to get over the hump, to feel as confident and cool as the other Dallas socialites I was seeing night after night. This was well before I understood that professional help was available. My problems just existed—I never thought there might be a plan available to diagnose and treat them in any formal way. The only way I knew how to "treat" them was to self-medicate with both legal and illegal substances. Soon, I'd find some more.

•

When I moved to Dallas I had only seen cocaine once in my life. At 16, I road-tripped with one of my buddies to his sister's place in West Virginia to spend New Year's Eve. I remember that they put this white powder out on the living room table. I had no idea what it was until they told me it was cocaine. I still had no idea what it was. I was from the suburbs of Pittsburgh, not hanging with the cocaine cowboys of Miami, Florida. When the cocaine was put in front of me in Morgantown, my friend's sister and her husband told me it would make feel good. My friend discouraged me from doing it, and, frankly, I was too scared. It never occurred to me as something to pursue, even as I cycled through other destructive behaviors during college and law school.

Summer, 1987. Hanging out on a Friday night at Beau Nash at the prestigious Crescent Hotel in Dallas with one of my best friends, Ethan. Ethan was also a lawyer and a real ladies' man. I met him at my gym. I was always hoping to become a ladies' man by osmosis when I hung out with him. Friday was the big night at Beau Nash. A who's who of the Dallas party scene. That night, Ethan asked me if I'd like to try cocaine. For the first time, I flashed back to Morgantown, West Virginia. I already had a few drinks in me, and I wanted so badly to be part of the cool Dallas scene. It only took me a millisecond to decide. While my buddy stood guard, I went into a bathroom stall.

I would soon become an expert in the "cocaine qualities" of bathroom stalls. There are good stalls and there are bad stalls to do cocaine in. Good stalls have actual doors that close tight. Bad stalls are the ones you see in most restaurant and club bathrooms—they have gaps on the sides of the doors where people can see in. Sometimes employees of clubs will take a peek around stall doors. I have known several people who have been busted for possession in that manner over the years. Of course, it became a trade skill to be able to do cocaine in pretty much any bathroom stall in any situation. I was a connoisseur of both cocaine and bathrooms—and I was proud of it. The crazy standards of an addict.

The downstairs bathroom at the Crescent Hotel was a good bathroom stall. I was able to snort my very first line of cocaine in perfect privacy. Within seconds, I was in heaven. I was suddenly the most handsome guy in the club, and I saw a confident, chiseled image in the bathroom mirror—the first time I saw the reflection of a coke addict. I had to have it again. Of course, at the same time, my throat became numb, and it became difficult to swallow. The panic started to overtake the cocaine-high confidence. Another snort was in order. Within moments, I had discovered the magic trick I needed to instantly transform myself from monster to man. I now knew the secret to defeating the body-dysmor-phia mindset. Cocaine was the answer. I knew, in the back of my mind, that I was adding two plus two and getting five, but I didn't care.

By the time I was in my late twenties, cocaine became a routine part of my life, like washing my socks. I was very aware of the illegality of the sub-stance, but, like most addicts, I never really cared about the consequences. Indeed, I never really thought I would get caught. I used in a very tight circle, but I did push the envelope more and more as my addiction got worse.

Ecstasy was also readily available, and it worked just as well as cocaine to make me feel like I'd turned from Mr. Hyde back to Dr. Jekyll. Ecstasy was an accepted "high society" drug along with co-caine. I actually preferred ecstasy because it was easier to obtain, hide, and ingest without detection. The downside was that you never really knew what was in the pill you were swallowing. I had heard hor-ror stories of people dropping dead after taking pills cut with rat poison and other lethal substances. I didn't care.

The effects lasted longer, and they were exactly what I thought I was looking for. They made me feel like a person who was self-confident, sexy, and out-going. I doubt, however, that sexy and self-confident was how others were actually seeing me at the time. I eventually shared a house with some friends I had met working for the city. We would throw monthly parties in what we had dubbed "the Checkerboard Club," so-called because the kitchen (which also served as the dance floor) had a black-and-white tile floor that looked like a checkerboard. Massive amounts of beer and cocaine were standard while "Pump Up the Volume" by MARRS blared over the stereo.

> *Pump up the volume! Shot Shot!*
> *Pump up the Volume! Snort Snort!*
> *Rock the House!*

A standard party was two kegs of beer, a trash can filled with Welch's Grape-Aid and Everclear grain alcohol, and, of course, as much cocaine as I could get my hands on. I was not making much money working for the city, but that did not stop me from spending it all on alcohol and drugs. Phone calls from the bill collectors were no problem. Not having money to purchase an eight-ball for one of the monthly parties was my only real worry.

Through all my coke use back then, it never entered my mind that any line could be my last lineor that my future legal career could be ruined. I wouldn't have cared. There was that damn incredible reflection in the bathroom mirror of Beau Nash. I had to have it again at all costs, even of my career and freedom.

•

Late summer, 1987. Two A.M. Just hit my one-year anniversary in Dallas. Night out at the new local sports bar, Legends. A boxing ring in the middle of the room with the tables surrounding the ring. Televisions ringing the room. Yuppies, pool sharks, and sports-team groupies. Pretty waitresses dressed as ring girls carrying around the latest knockout potions.

There she is. Tall and pretty, another classic Dallas blonde. My brainwaves start short-circuiting. Memories of the freshman Penn State redhead flood my thoughts. Despite my obsessive self-doubt, I am talkative, aggressive, and confident, at least until the coke wears off. A conversation of lies. To tell the truth is to face the truth about myself. What is that dribbling down the side of my chin? The cocaine has frozen my throat muscles. With every lie I tell, spit either drools out of my mouth or, like a projectile, finds its way onto her arm. I can see my reflection on the glossy marble tabletop. I look like I have rabies.

"Are you okay?" she asks. "You keep spitting on me!"

"I'm sorry, I didn't realize I was doing that. So, do you like Billy Joel?" I ask. "We should go see him in concert the next time he's in Dallas." Had to get that out before the cocaine wore off. I manage to get her number somehow.

Then, out into the night. It's early morning and nearly autumn, but it still feels like 100 degrees. The lack of breeze is stifling. I am sweating, as damp as if I had just stepped out of the shower. Not sure if it's the humidity or the three huge lines I just did. Cocaine is my lunch and breakfast, with tequila on the side. I have not eaten all day. I did get in my twelve-mile run. I'm feeling a little like I'm having a bad high. Edgy. Lock-jawed. Maybe I bought some bad shit. Have to find a new dealer. Then again, maybe the next lines will be better.

I hop in my buddy's car and we head to Mickey D's, where I grab five Egg McMuffins with bacon and cheese. We pull up in front of my apartment. Door opens. I step out of the passenger side and into the street.

Suddenly I am airborne! Feet taken out from under me. I am propelled into a full somersault, a death grip on my McDonald's bag. Boom! I slam down on the windshield of a passing car with bone-jarring force. What the hell happened? Where did this car come from? The windshield shatters. It releases from its frame and drops into the vehicle. I'm on the hood of the car and I have a McMuffin in my mouth. My buddy is driving on down the road, oblivious to my street acrobatics. I roll off the hood and onto the street. A man is standing over me. He's shouting at me. I'm laughing. I notice that my white polo shirt is soaked in blood. A woman starts screaming at me.

"YOU WALKED IN FRONT OF US! CALL THE POLICE!"
I am still laughing at my airborne somersault. Maybe
it's the cocaine.

"Get back in the car!" the man yells at the woman. Then they're gone.

I am still lying in the street amid the broken
windshield glass. A lot of blood is coming from
somewhere. I peel myself off the hot asphalt and
hobble into the apartment. Check the mirror. Lots of
cuts and bruises. Some cocaine left in my pocket. No
biggie. Still have my Egg McMuffins. Shower, change,
sniff, shot, binge, puke. Just another night in Dallas,
Texas. Add in three broken ribs. Do another line—
that'll make those ribs feel better. Calling the blonde.
Damn. She gave me a phony number. I would have
done the same if I were her.

Next.

•

November 27, 1987. Two months after I was
hit by that car, I hadn't slowed down. I met some
friends for happy hour at On The Border in Dallas.
I had a huge crush on one of them—from afar, as
always. She had actually made some effort to establish a friendship as my running partner. In my usual
method of operation, the only way I could muster
the courage to ask her out was to get drunk, which I
did. I could not get one word out of my mouth. I was

too scared. Terrified that she would see who I really was when the alcohol bravado wore off.

I went home upset. I yanked open the refrigerator and pulled out the tofu turkey my mother had sent me for Thanksgiving. I ate it all. I purged it all. The phone rang. It was my best friend and roommate. He knew how I was. That I would often isolate myself when depressed. After some prodding, he convinced me to head out with some friends to our favorite nightclub, Fast and Cool. After just purging my meal, I was not really in a mood to put myself through the same misery that I had experienced a couple hours earlier at happy hour. More women, more alcohol. More depression. More self-hatred.

But I drank some tequila to get the buzz back, and I was ready to go. I knew that sitting at home would sink me into a deeper depression. So why not take another shot at glory? It was a common theme in my life. So I went out. That night I met my first wife.

I met her in the normal manner in which I met most of my dates—while drunk and high. She was a very pretty woman from a small town in West Texas. I was fascinated with her local accent, a particular Texas twang that I had never heard before. When I gave her an alcohol-aided goodnight kiss, she was only the third woman I had kissed in my life.

We got married in 1988. We were divorced in 1990. In reality, neither of us was ready to marry.

Ours followed a pattern I see in many young marriages. Nothing changes. Drinking and nights out single become drinking and nights out married. You basically become roommates. She didn't do drugs. While I did not use as heavily as I would after our divorce, I'd still do cocaine when I went out partying without her, and I hid that aspect of my life from her. I would soon look forward to our designated Thursday "single night's" when we would go out separately with our friends. It was my chance to do drugs.

Eventually, I would come to hate those Thursday nights. They were a reminder that I had failed, that nothing had changed in my life. That our marriage was failing. I felt the first tugs of awareness that I had become a full-blown addict, unable to move on from the coke and alcohol that were ruining my relationship. But I wasn't motivated to change. It seemed so normal in Dallas. Most people that I hung around with were doing it. I wasn't ready to find help, least of all from my wife, from whom I was hiding so much. We never had a chance.

My first marriage would set the pattern for future relationships. Initially, they'd offer some relief from destructive patterns of addiction and eating disorders. Then they'd end, and I'd return to partying, drugs, and alcohol. I made some attempts at counseling and dealing with the depression that I had dealt with most of my life, but it was all superficial. All of it was a Band-Aid. None of it revolved around knowledge of BDD or any kind of honesty about my thoughts, feelings, and memories. That was still decades away. I'd go to therapists and lament how depressed I was, without ever talking about the core of my problems. I'd never talk about my childhood and/or my relationship with my mother. I wouldn't tell my therapist about the drugs and drinking. I'd never tell them about my obsessive thoughts about my looks and body, the extreme eating behaviors. I'd never tell them about my actual problems, and so I never gave them a chance to do their jobs.

After my marriage ended, my behavior became increasingly desperate, self-destructive, and bizarre. I can remember times when I would buy a pizza, eat a slice, then throw the rest in a trash bin outside the pizza joint out of shame. Two hours later, after a seemingly endless string of obsessive, self-loathing thoughts, I'd go dig the old pizza out of the trash bin, flies and everything, clean it off, stick it in the microwave and eat it. I'd then feel the disgust of what I had just done and purge it. The return of bulimic behavior was like a warm security blanket.

•

Summer, 1990. Every teen who gets drunk for the first time should be forced to spend a night in the drunk tank of a major city jail. Pardon the pun, but it is a sobering experience. I know. I spent my night.

I had gotten divorced from my first wife in January of 1990 and had been on a subsequent cocaine and alcohol binge. There is always an excuse for an addict. I was drinking at a bar called The Gingerman. It's a place that specializes in fancy beers sold in enormous beer mugs. After getting sufficiently sloshed on giant beers by about 1 A.M., I started feeling sorry for myself and decided to head home. I was flying up the Dallas North Tollway at about 75 mph. I was about ¼ mile from the house where I lived with Mark when I passed a state trooper. I knew immediately he had me, and, sure enough, the lights came on, and he pulled me over within walking distance from my house. After the roadside test, he told me I was being arrested on suspicion of DWI and slapped the cuffs on me. He was a nice, older guy who even pulled over to loosen my cuffs when I told him they were cutting into my wrists. We carried on a pleasant conversation the entire trip to the Lew Sterrett jail, which is the main jail and holding facility for the city of Dallas. I asked him if he would take me back to my car when I blew under .10 (the legal limit in 1990). He laughed and said that he didn't think that was going to be the case, but if they didn't book me, they would take me back. He was right. I blew a .11 on the Breathalyzer. I failed to follow the advice I always gave others: Don't blow. But like any real drunk, I had convinced myself I was not drunk.

I thought being handcuffed on the side of a public highway was humiliating. It was nothing compared to the assembly-line booking process. A long row of fingerprinting and abuse from the local deputy sheriffs handling the process. Rightfully so. It was open season. One of them leaned across the table, his face inches from my nose, and starting yelling for all to hear:

"YOU'RE A STINKING LAWYER? ONE THING IS FOR SURE. YOU DO STINK! YOU ARE A DISGRACE TO THE LEGAL PROFESSION! I HOPE THEY KICK YOU OUT!"

I agreed with him. I didn't say a word. I believed that I fully deserved the abuse and that it was part of my punishment. It was no fun at all. It should have been a learning experience. It was not. Like many addicts who are humiliated, repentant, and swear off drinking, drugs, or whatever else in the immediate aftermath, the further the event was removed in time, the more the humiliation subsided, and the easier it was to tell myself it would never happen again and move right back into my old ways.

Perhaps it didn't help that I ended up beating the rap. I pled not guilty. I chose to try the case, and I was lucky. The state trooper did not show up for trial, so they had to dismiss the charges. I heard through the grapevine that he had retired and didn't feel like dealing with it.

I remember my attorney handing me the dismissal. When I thanked him, he said to thank the district attorney for dismissing the case. I had no idea he was being tongue-in-cheek. I stuck my head in the office next to the courtroom and said, "Thank you." They were not amused. Their expressions told me I should have humbly stayed quiet. I high-tailed it out of the courthouse before they changed their minds. I gave no thought to how I had gotten to that point. No thought of maybe needing help for an alcohol-and-drug problem. Just relief that I had dodged a bullet. No hard consequences other than the few grand I gave my lawyer and getting my car out of impoundment. I stayed sober for about two weeks after I got out of jail.

•

Beating the three-headed beast of addiction, eating disorders, and BDD is a huge challenge. Alcohol and cocaine can create physical dependency, meaning the body goes through withdrawal symptoms when the abused substance is no longer present in the body. But for me, more than the physical addiction, crutches like alcohol and cocaine created an emotional dependency in that they helped me feel like a new person and escape a deeply degraded sense of self. The binging and purging also created an emotional dependency, helping me release the shame of not being able to change what I saw in the mirror every morning.

Of course, it only creates more shame. This is the spinning wheel of BDD—I was like a gerbil running endlessly, looking for that one fix that would make me feel good about myself. It was always easier to choose the destructive behavior. This has been the harder problem to overcome. I did not always feel the need to do cocaine or even drink. Whether it was alcohol, cocaine, or binging and purging, I was always most addicted to the ability to change how I felt about myself simply by turning the wheel. As with other grave symptoms of BDD, I learned how to put addictions and eating disorders behind me only when I learned to address the root causes of my dysfunction.

But I wouldn't learn that important lesson for years, for decades. For me, I always thought salvation was around the corner—lose one more pound, go to one more party, find one more woman who might tell me she loved me. For so many years, I thought the trick to solving my problems was simply figuring out how to be more of a manly man. Unfortunately, I found another destructive behavior in the wheel to help with this.

# CHAPTER 5:
## *Confessions of a Steroid Monster*

*Jacked-up on steroids.*

*I* am dreaming of needles. I'm in a gym full of people from my past. They are all staring at me as I walk in. I notice my pants are down. I am walking with them around my ankles. Everyone is still staring. I can't pull them up! I feel sickened. The floor is covered with syringes. I am walking on my toes trying not to get pricked. I pick up a syringe. If I can shoot up, the people will stop staring. Where are my clean needles?

Suddenly, I am in my bedroom as a child. I am looking in the attic. There is my box of syringes and steroids. It's just out of reach. My child's outstretched arms just can't seem to reach the shoebox full of every kind of steroid imaginable. Finally I'm able to grab hold of the box. I pull it down and sit on my bed. The vials appear empty. I try to take the wrapper off the syringe. It won't come off. The harder I try to unwrap the syringe, the tougher it is to get off. My hands are rubbery, numb. I realize it doesn't matter: I am still a child, and the steroids can't help me become a man. Maybe, next time, the vials will be full. Everything will change for the better.

•

For those unfamiliar with anabolic steroids, they can make you bigger, faster, and stronger. It's not a myth. If you follow bodybuilding, professional baseball or football, or many other sports, you know what I am talking about. In bodybuilding and professional sports, steroids are used with a specific purpose in mind. They can elevate performance, accelerate recovery from injury, or change physical appearance and, thereby, make the user more money in a given profession. On the other end of the spectrum, there are those who use steroids for reasons that have nothing to do with making money or competing on a professional level. Some people use and abuse steroids for the sole purpose of looking better, being more popular, and feeling better about themselves. Steroids can be psychologically addictive for that very reason.

For the most part, anabolic steroids are not legal to purchase or use. However, some anabolics

have legal, limited medical uses, and synthetic testosterone is sometimes prescribed to men with low
natural testosterone. They also have documented
side effects. According to the National Institute on
Drug Abuse, anabolic steroids are associated with
a range of side effects and health risks for men, including male-pattern baldness, acne, and breast de-
velopment in men, as well as heart disease and liver
cancer. Steroids use has also been linked to heart ar-
rhythmia and, particularly, atrial fibrillation, which
I suffer from and for which I have been hospitalized
three times. Discontinuing steroid use did not solve
that problem. Like the Jam-of-the-Month Club, steroid abuse is a gift that keeps on giving.

For men young and old, anabolic steroids can
seem like a perfect solution for improving self-image. Steroids can make insecure young men feel mature and virile and insecure aging men feel young
and virile. Men can feel like they are transforming
into one of those airbrushed media images of body-
builders or shirtless movie stars with hot women on
each arm. If they can be that, they can have it all.
Of course, abuse of steroids is not limited to men.
I have personally known women who have abused
anabolic steroids for fitness, competition, or just to
look better.

Summer, 1985. I was first introduced to steroids when an acquaintance asked me to inject him
in the butt with a steroid called Equipoise, a drug

commonly used on horses. I had driven to Dallas to visit my brother with a guy I had met in a Pittsburgh weight room. His name was Sean Stopperich. Sean was a huge guy and was one of the key players in the Southern Methodist University Football Program receiving the "death penalty" in 1987 for paying players, among other violations.

I wanted to visit both of my brothers, who were living in Dallas, and Sean wanted to visit some old friends of his from the team. I had not yet graduated from law school but was thinking about an eventual move. He volunteered to drive us. One morning, Sean and I were sitting in the living room of my brother's home, where we were staying during our visit. Sean opened a paper bag and pulled out a vial and syringe.

"Hey, bro, want to inject me?"

"Inject you? Are you a diabetic?"

"No—roids, man! Equipoise! It's a horse steroid. I need you to inject me in my butt. I can do it myself, but it's easier if someone else does it." He pulled out a vial and a couple of syringes. My stomach got queasy.

"Horses? You have to be shitting me. And, no, I'm not sticking a needle in your butt. I'm not going anywhere near your butt."

"No, dude! This is how it's done. I used this all through college."

"Whatever works for you. Stick your own butt.

I'm going for a run."

He dropped his shorts and bent over, craning his neck to see his rear end. He said, "Brian, you're a skinny guy. If you want to put on some size and be popular with the ladies, watch and learn. Dallas women like big dudes."

Then he did something I would learn how to do myself years later. He stuck that big needle in his butt cheek, pulled up his pants, and headed straight off to the gym.

I was surprised by what I saw Sean do, but also fascinated. He performed the ritual so smoothly and casually; it seemed like just a typical step in a work-out routine for a seriously fit guy, like stretching or making sure to drink plenty of fluids. There was no shame in his dropping his shorts to expose himself to me. It was like getting up to brush your teeth every morning. His routine would become my own. Pull out the cotton alcohol swabbing pads. Be sure to have two needles, one for drawing out the steroids, and one for injecting them. This is to prevent contamination and possible infection. Clean the injection area. Inject with an 18-gauge needle. On with the day.

Sadly, Sean died in 1995 of a suspected drug overdose. Like me and many other recreational steroid users, the abuse of bodybuilding substances went hand in hand with the use of other illicit substances.

I had no real desire to take steroids after seeing what Sean did, but my attitude began to change when I permanently relocated to Dallas. Sean's words in that living room stuck with me. Dallas women like big dudes.

When I moved to Dallas on Labor Day of 1986, it was a new ball game, with different rules of conduct. It seemed like everyone I saw was fit, beautiful, young, and just looking for fun and adventure. I was coming from a place where fun and adventure meant running alone for hours each day, getting drunk alone, binging on fast food, purging it, and obsessing about my love handles and receding hairline. What I was seeing blew my mind, but I had absolutely no self-confidence to join the big Texas party. At least not without taking even more drastic measures. It couldn't just be about being thin anymore. These women weren't after marathon runners. I had to be a muscular dude.

In 1986, you could obtain certain types of anabolic steroids legally with a prescription. I was working out at a now-defunct gym called the Body Forum in Dallas. One of my workout partners was a guy named Jeff Gaylord. Jeff was an All-America football player at the University of Missouri. For a long time, he held the college-conference bench-press record. (He went on to become a pro wrestler, teaming up with Sidney "Sid Vicious" Eudy, and then ended up convicted of bank robbery in Colorado.)

Steroid use at the Body Forum was open and rampant. Guys would bring their "works" into the gym— their syringes, vials of whatever anabolic injectable liquids they were cycling on, and their pills. It was not uncommon to see "roid monsters" shoot up in the locker room. You'd see them in open bathroom stalls, standing up, bent over with their workout shorts dropped to their ankles. They were all huge, muscular, ripped. They were always talking about working out or getting pretty girls. It played right into my body dysmorphia. I wanted to be those guys when I looked in the mirror. I wanted to see what they saw! I wanted to see that handsome, sexy, intelligent, in-shape guy that I had not once seen since the day I was born. There was no doubt in my mind that adding steroids to the mix would solve all my self-image problems.

I had no concept of the dangers of steroids at that time, but, even if I had been aware, it would have made no difference. Times had changed since I watched Sean Stopperich shoot up my in my brother's living room. I had to walk the walk if I wanted to be accepted in my new town. I embraced steroids with the all-in enthusiasm of that eighteen-year-old freshman who had embraced self-starvation. Screw those needles, though! After uncomfortably watching Sean Stopperich inject himself, I decided that pills were the best route for me.

I asked Jeff Gaylord about the best way to go

about getting the roids. I was given the name of a
doctor in Fort Worth, Texas, who would prescribe
steroids as part of a "weight gain" program. I made
the appointment, got my physical, and received my
prescription for the steroid Anavar. Anavar is a fairly
low-impact anabolic steroid taken orally as a pill. It
can help add lean muscle mass. Like many steroids,
however, it could be dangerous in combination with
other substances such as alcohol. Anabolics can
cause significant liver damage when mixed with
drinking, and, though I was warned by the doctor,
I continued to drink heavily and even use cocaine
while on Anavar. I got a prescription for a ten-week
supply, and it worked quickly. I went from 185 to 200
pounds in a few months. The problem was that damn
mirror. Even as I put on lean muscle mass, I saw a fat
kid. I saw huge love handles. Even as people compli-
mented me, I was awash in muscle dysmorphic self-
doubt. Muscle dysmorphia is a type of BDD in which
the sufferer becomes obsessively preoccupied with
his or her degree of muscularity. Like other aspects
of BDD, it can lead to impaired social and occupa-
tional functioning, and, as with me, steroid abuse.

Steroids became a regular tool in constructing
my artificial sense of self-worth. I wrestled with my
self-image and tried to convince myself that I should
believe what others told me about my body. And it
worked, for a time. I dated. I met my first wife. And,
when things were good, I didn't feel the need to use

steroids as much. Not long after our engagement, my wife and I began fighting a lot over very small things, and sometimes I'd fly into rages. I began doing some research on the side effects and first became acquainted with the term "roid rage." I had no idea if that was the problem, but our relationship was very rocky at that point. I decided that the Anavar could be part of the problem. I took the pills to work with me and flushed them down the toilet. That was the last time I would use steroids for many years. When I eventually went back to them, it would be with even more disastrous results.

What would I use to replace the self-image void left when I stopped roiding? What was my next choice on the spinning behavior wheel? I had someone who loved me, and I felt desired. For a time, those feelings displaced my need for steroids. While I had not completely given up cocaine, I left much of the party scene behind. But good times never seem to last long. When you're an addict—whether it be steroids, alcohol, or drugs—stopping their use does not solve the underlying problems that drove you to substance abuse in the first place. Even though I had someone who constantly reassured me as I expressed self-doubts about my body, it lasted only until the next time I scrutinized my image in my bathroom mirror, a reflective window at the mall, or even in my rearview mirror as I drove.

When that marriage failed in 1990, I decided

that the quickest way back to the top of the pyramid on the Dallas party scene was another steroid cycle. Unfortunately, for me, anabolic steroids had become illegal for my purposes. Having no legitimate means to obtain them and not yet being aware of the black market, I had to be content with hard work in the gym.

I also quickly fell back into old coping habits that made me feel better about myself. Every night, I went to a different bar. I had developed several cocaine connections and began using it at an unprecedented level. I spent every weekend obtaining it and getting hammered. No steroids meant I was back to running long distances as well. Running was a familiar comfort to me. It allowed me to once again isolate myself and fuel my obsessive-compulsive exercise desires. One foot in front of the other. Every day. Every mile. Every moment.

Back in that mindset, I also returned to binging and purging. Memories of Penn State, peanut M&M's, and pizza. Body image run amok. Time run amok. Moving in the wrong direction—back to familiar destructive behaviors and failed relationships. Falling further into the abyss. Not caring if I ever hit bottom.

•

Summer, 1998. Sitting at the pool at the Hard

Rock Hotel and Casino in Las Vegas. It is a beautiful, sunny, summer day. Blazing hot. Eggs-frying-on-the-sidewalk hot. The cloudless sky looks like it could stretch all the way back to Dallas. I love Vegas. I can get drunk, do cocaine, and be the Brian I want to be. And the Hard Rock pool is the place to be. Beautiful people all around me, with muscles and flat, six-pack stomachs. Everyone having fun.

I, however, am alone, thinking about my second failed marriage, fading in my rearview mirror. The divorce was finalized in June. On my own again, the urge returned to be one of those beautiful people. They say what happens in Vegas stays in Vegas, but the reverse is definitely not true: you can't escape the truth by running to the desert. And I still haven't confronted the truth.

I'm sitting on the edge of the pool as the oven-hot sun burns my pale, bare shoulders exposed by my muscle shirt. But I won't take my shirt off—I can't possibly take it off. I am still not perfect, not like these people. My arms drop to my sides. I fold them in front of me, reflexively covering my gut that is already covered by my shirt. I subtly push back on my stomach, hoping that if I flatten it, it will look better, and I can take my shirt off. My hands move to my sides to pinch the fat on my love handles. Have they grown any since I checked this morning? I haven't eaten yet, so they should be okay. Push in on them. Into my sides, flattening, hoping they don't bounce back. Pulling up my shorts over my belly button so I can create the illusion of a flat stomach.

Shirt finally comes off. Into the pool. In my mind, everyone's attention instantly turns to me. My brain tells me they're laughing. What are they laughing at? I should look good. I even purged the night before. I have not eaten today. I feel their eyes following me as I retreat to a corner of the pool and cover my stomach again with my arms. Why should other people's opinions bother me? There are people starving and dying all over the world, and here I am, obsessed with my gut. I never took the time to think seriously about that question. I lay out in the sun. I feel better for a moment because lying down, my stomach doesn't bulge. A relieved feeling. But the false thoughts born of BDD quickly return. I need a drink, I thought. I need a bump. I head back to my room and decide I will never take my shirt off in public again. The pool is the ultimate "shirts and skins." The shirts are losers. I hate the pool.

In 1998, I was developing new obsessions about my appearance. Not only was I still at war with my waistline and convinced I wasn't attractive enough, I also had the early effects of aging to contend with. Muscle mass was becoming harder to add naturally. Tiny wrinkles were starting to form around my eyes. And my hairline was receding. All the normal by-products of aging but magnified and distorted by my mind.

I can't say when my fixation on my hairline reached the tipping point. It was more like a building tsunami of obsessive-compulsive thoughts about my impending inevitable baldness. My dad is almost completely bald. His dad was bald. My mom's dad was bald. I didn't have to be a member of MENSA (I'm not) to predict my genetic destiny. Soon those feelings became obsessive and compulsive. I began contemplating new forms of body modification. Surgery is expensive but instantaneous, a radical way to transform the image in the mirror in a single day. Body modification is quite common for those with body dysmorphic disorder, and, in my case, it resulted in hair transplants and one expensive liposuction treatment. Of course, I've been tempted throughout my adulthood to try even more. The thoughts still come; it's how I process them that makes the difference.

Soon, I'd begin the first of three hair-transplant procedures. I was willing to spend whatever amount it would take to cover each bald spot on my head. Looking in the mirror, I would experiment endlessly, trying to find the optimum angle for holding my head to make it look like I had hair. I would fixate on my hair in my rearview mirror when I should have been looking in front of me driving down the road—more than once forcing me to hit the brakes or swerve into another lane to keep from hitting another car.

At the doctor's office, while signing up for my first procedure, there was a cursory psychological questionnaire to identify my motives for wanting surgery. I didn't understand then that the questionnaire was intended to weed out patients with an obsessive-compulsive desire to have multiple plastic surgeries. Someone not psychologically fit for the procedure. Someone doing it for the wrong reasons. Someone like me. I certainly would not have responded that I saw a monster in the mirror and would continue to engage in surgical procedures until I no longer saw that creature. I told them what they wanted to hear. I simply wanted to improve my appearance.

The procedures themselves were relatively painless. They put me half-under with a Demerol drip, took some hair from the back of my head, and transplanted it up front, where my hair was thinning. It takes about six months for the new hair to come in. All I could think about during those six months was getting the next procedure. I was determined to have a full head of hair. But even that wasn't enough. What about those damn love handles, though? I can't cover them up with hair! I need to do more.

•

Fall, 1998. Another season of discontent. After my second divorce, my life is once again in do-over mode. Have to meet someone! Have to get back in shape! Have to once again grasp for the unattainable. The ebb and flow of obsessive-compulsive behavior is in the forefront once again. The triggers are numerous and predictable. The mirror in my bathroom. The reflection in the store windows in the local mall. The reflection on my computer monitor. The need to be wanted by someone. The behavior wheel is once again spinning. Where will it stop? I join a popular "singles" health club in Dallas where there are lots of beautiful women. And then there's something I haven't seen in a while: steroids! Yeah, baby! Not something talked about much around a yuppie gym, but if you're looking and listening for the right words and phrases, you get a good feel for who is juicing. Steroids are illegal, but I don't care. The risk is a distant, secondary consideration to the high: The high of ripped muscles, of being told I'm looking good, of being glanced at by females. I made my first black-market-steroids purchase that year.

Upon recommendation of a person at my gym, I obtained the steroids Primobolan, Deca-Durabolin ("Deca"), and Winstrol. Deca is a very popular injectable steroid that can build muscle mass very quickly. As compared to other anabolic steroids, the side effects, when Deca is used in moderation, are not that severe. At my steroid-monster worst, I was injecting about 400mg per week. Primobolan and Winstrol do not equate to the dramatic size gains of Deca. I used them to gain lean muscle mass and lose body fat. My steroid cycles would generally last eight to ten weeks, with a few months off. It was not scientific. Guys in the know at my gym would tell me stuff about different types of steroids and cycles. I would go on the Internet and do my research. I would call my connection, and, a couple weeks later, at a meeting for lunch or coffee, the dealer would slide a brown bag over to me under the table.

At the start, I had never injected myself with anything in my life. I was no big fan of the sight of my own blood. The thought of putting a one- or two-inch needle into my butt twice a week, the ritual I had seen Sean perform years earlier, made my stomach turn. I had seen others use a mirror, but I could not bring myself to do that. Mirrors were a deal breaker. I learned the hard way, simply twisting my torso and head to the right or left, depending on which side I was injecting. I would stick myself standing up. After a lot of trial and error, I got it down pretty well. There were a few times when I would hit a vein, and the blood would spurt a foot across the room. This is a common occurrence for grown-up steroid monsters, but, even at nearly forty years old, I was a steroid baby, and it scared me shitless. When I complained that my butt felt like a pincushion, the person who mentored me told me that I should start injecting into my quadriceps.

The worst part of the steroid cycle was when I

would stop using for any given period of time either in between cycles or because I couldn't afford them. My artificially escalated testosterone would plummet while my body fought to get back in its own rhythm of testosterone production. This equated to chemical depression stacked on top of my already existing clinical depressive state, lethargy, and lack of sex drive. I would miss that feeling of having hard muscles all the time. Unable to take steroids because I was either in between a cycle or broke, I'd start lifting heavier weight to compensate. Day in and day out, twice a day. I went from 200 to 230 pounds in a little more than three months.

Like every other destructive behavior, the obsessive-compulsive element to my steroid use was overwhelming. I was constantly fixated on the next injection. I would imagine the gains and confidence that would come from getting stronger. I'd create vivid, life-like scenarios in my mind of social acceptance and popularity. I could play my entire life from injection to old age and get a sense of relief that everything would be okay after that next injection. Like my extreme dieting, I never felt I had done quite enough. The next injection will be the one that gets me where I want, I'd think.

As with my cosmetic surgeries, steroid addiction has a financial component. It is expensive to buy illegal drugs on the black market. During the full spectrum of my steroid use, starting from my first pill to the last injection over the course of my life, I estimate that I spent approximately $10,000 on my addiction. In comparative terms for other "recreational steroid addicts," that is actually not a bad figure, but, combined with the surgeries, I was spending more money than I had on fixes that would never make me feel good enough.

•

Spring, 1999. Once again standing in the office of my plastic surgeon. The damn love handles are killing me. They're holding me back! In my mind, a saggy waistline is preventing me from doing everything I know I am capable of. I have to get rid of them. I have that four grand available on my credit card, just barely enough to cover it.

"Please strip naked, Brian."

"Do I get a gown?"

"No, we need you completely naked. We need to photograph you before and after the liposuction procedure and paint you with iodine."

Naked?? My body temperature rises 10 degrees.

They're staring at my ugly body!

They're whispering to each other!

They're laughing at me, I can see it!

Cover up!

I move my hands in front of my stomach, trying to cover it and my love handles as much as I can.

The fact that my genitals are exposed doesn't even register. That doesn't embarrass me.

"Brian, please move your hands away—we need a clear photograph." This would be a lot easier if I had a bump of coke, I think.

In the end, removing some of the love handles didn't solve anything. I'd still notice sagging around my waist. I was fat even when I was thin. In my mind, if I could drop those love handles, I would lose another belt notch. What would that have gotten me? Maybe a path to another surgery and another belt notch. Then another and another. In reality, my belt notches were fine. It didn't matter.

The hair transplants did what they were supposed to do: I had more hair. But it wasn't enough. Even today, I sometimes think about it. All I need is one more hair transplant, and then . . .

The difference is that, today, while I may think about it, I remind myself that I am fine the way I am. There's no reason to have surgery.

Here is what I have concluded in the process of leaving the child behind and becoming a man: Whatever people may or may not be thinking about my hair or my baldness, my desirability based on baldness has nothing to do with me. It has to do with that child who wanted so badly to be accepted. For me, one key to overcoming my obsessive thoughts has been to keep that child in mind always and to remind him—and myself—that I can love and be loved.

•

December 20, 2000. I'm going on a cruise with my father! We're headed to Asia. Our journey will take us to Singapore, Bali, Bangkok, and Hong Kong. I am becoming increasingly pre-occupied with the thought of my father's advancing age and mortality. I want to spend time with him. My father and I have never traveled by ourselves before. I'm so excited!

Now dating the woman who will become my third wife, I have stopped using cocaine, but I am abusing steroids heavily. Even with the anticipation of the cruise, I am thinking intensely of my self-image. I imagine all the new people I'll meet on the cruise ship. People who will be impressed by how ripped I am. They will accept me.

I fly into L.A. early to meet my dad. From there we will catch our flight to Singapore. I smuggled my steroids and works on the plane and planned to use them up at a Los Angeles gym before we head overseas. I find a gym and shoot up two weeks' worth of Deca and Sustanon. I work out like a mad man. If I can just put on these last few millimeters of muscle before we step on the boat, I will have a chance to be a new man among new, admiring friends.

After a night in Singapore, we get on the boat,

*All smiles with my father in Bangkok.*

and, in my mind, everyone is checking me out. But it isn't because of my muscles. It's because, at thirty-nine, I'm one of the youngest people on the cruise. The faces turned toward me are all well past middle-age—this is a cruise for retirees. They don't care about my looks—they're just wondering what I'm doing on the boat.

Once in our cabin, I rage at my father. I want to go home. "Why did you choose a cruise with all geriatrics?" I demand. "Who am I going to talk to? Who will want to talk to me?"

My father is bewildered. This cruise was not intended to be a big social occasion. It was about spending time with his son. This was sitting with him at Forbes Field for his first baseball game. Sitting facing me, with the ocean stretched out behind him, he began to cry. "I'm sorry—I failed you," he said. He lived his life for his sons. He just wants me to be happy, to enjoy myself. In his mind, he has failed.

In reality, I have just experienced one of the biggest life failures of my existence. I have made my father weep with my selfishness. I'm a prick who has just bullied his father.

I don't think the memory of my father crying will ever leave me. My father's pain is my pain. The upside is that when I think back to that moment, it is an anchor to remember the person I had become. Having a clear vision of those times is essential to reminding me how unhealthy and destructive behaviors can affect family and relationships. For me, hurting my father was the worst thing possible. I use it as a springboard for making better decisions when dealing with those I love and want to please.

Still using steroids after the cruise, I made what was almost a tragic mistake. In February of 2001, I accidentally injected myself in the quadriceps with the same needle I had used to inject another part of my body. (I otherwise always used a new syringe to maintain a sterile environment.) I had forgotten to throw one of the needles away and confused it with the sterile one. This transferred the bacteria on the needle from the first injection to the new puncture in my quad. When the new puncture closed, it created the perfect environment for a staph infection.

I first noticed the aching in my left leg around April of that year. I did not pay much attention to it. I was working out hard twice a day and thought I had pulled a muscle. The quadriceps began to swell, and, by July, it was getting difficult even to contract it. I finally went to my physician, and he recommended an MRI. He also prescribed antibiotics. I waited for the results, thinking that at worst, I had torn a quad muscle. I was in Pittsburgh visiting my parents when my doctor called me on my cell phone. There was panic and urgency in his voice.

"Brian, this is Dr. McNally, I have your MRI back. Where are you?"

"I'm in Pittsburgh, doc. What's up?"

"Is there a hospital close by?"

"Sure, St. Clair Hospital is right down the street."

"Check yourself in immediately! I'll contact them and explain the situation."

Now I was the one sounding panicked. "Doctor, exactly what is the situation?"

"You have a massive infection from just above your left knee working its way up toward your pelvis. We have to stop it immediately, or you could lose your leg." He again advised me to get to the nearest hospital.

But I didn't check myself into the hospital. I didn't want my parents or girlfriend to know that I was abusing steroids. It would be easier to lie about it and deal with in Dallas. Ignoring his dire warning, I flew back to Dallas that next morning and checked myself into the hospital there. I was immediately taken into surgery. The surgeon told me they were going to stick a twelve-inch syringe in my leg and see what came out. They would then decide whether to operate. The next thing I knew, it was eight hours later. They had cut my leg open and removed a massive abscess. I was told that if I had let it go one more week, I may have lost my leg. While I had told the doctor and the hospital what happened, I was in no mood to admit illegal steroid use to the people close to me. I told my girlfriend and family that I had fallen on a piece of metal at the gym that had punctured my leg and caused the infection.

The recovery was brutal. After a week in the hospital, I was discharged. But, first, the doctors inserted a tube into my body so that I could continue to administer antibiotics directly to the former site of the infection. The tube entered through my collarbone and went all the way down to my leg.

The insertion of the tube to carry the antibiotics required an operation in itself. They laid me flat on my back with my arms extended straight out to my sides, palms up. This was done under a local anesthetic. By the time the procedure was over, I could no longer feel my left arm. It was gone. Like it was no longer there. I panicked. "Doctor, I can't feel my left arm. What's wrong?!"

The doctor said in a matter-of-fact monotone, "Well, it could be one of three things. We accidently cut a nerve and you will never get the feeling back.

Or we nicked a nerve, and the feeling may come back eventually, but we can't say when. Or, your arm was just in an awkward position during the operation, and the feeling should come back quickly." I started bawling on the operating table before he even finished. Fortunately, it was door number three. The feeling came back.

When I was released from the hospital, I was given these little spherical containers of antibiotics that I would attach to the exposed end of the tube that protruded from a hole near my shoulder. The tube pumped strong antibiotics directly to the infected area with the aid of gravity. It was gross and painful. After about ten days with the antibiotic balls, I went back to the hospital, and they yanked out the tube. It really was a yank. Just pulled it right on out through the hole in my shoulder. I could feel it snaking back up through my body.

It took six months of rehabilitation to break the scar tissue and regain full range of movement in my leg. They cut so much muscle out of my left thigh that, today, I can still stick my finger deep into the scar area. My leg numbs up in that area if I exert it too much.

I consider myself lucky. Though it's not as publicized as other kinds of addiction, steroid dependency is associated with many health complications that can be fatal, including heart attacks, strokes, and liver tumors. Still, as close as I came to disaster,

I learned nothing. Almost losing my leg would turn out to be just one more low moment that did nothing to change my habits. I continued to use steroids. All my attempts at body modification were ultimately failures. Steroids made me stronger, hair replacement made me look more youthful, and liposuction temporarily made me skinny again. But just like purging, extreme exercise, drinking, and cocaine use, no change would ever be final enough for me to stop considering radical ways to transform myself.

Of course, my mistake was trying to change the way I appeared. I should have been trying to change the way I thought about myself, my needs, and my goals. Steroids, drug addiction, and body-modification surgeries have cost me both physically and financially. I have a permanent heart condition called atrial fibrillation, thanks to either the eating disorders, steroids, cocaine abuse, or the combination of all three. I have been hospitalized three times as a result. There is no telling how many years I have shortened my life because of my dangerous habits.

There is a lot of debate about the use of ster-oids, especially in the professional-sports arena. I make no judgments on that. What I can say is that, in my personal experience, very few of the people I knew who were using steroids were doing it for a professional reason. I know athletes who have used them. I know personal trainers who use them because they believe part of their monetary value is based on how good they look. The rest? I have no doubt that some are like me. Riding that dangerous thought process: If I can just get a little bit bigger, then I'll be attractive. I'll be accepted. I won't be bullied. I'll get the girl. The tradeoff for all those thoughts is the undeniable fact that they take a tremendous toll on the body. I'd give anything to have those years and my healthy heart and fully working leg back. Remember that when you make your choice.

# CHAPTER 6:

## *Marriage, Divorce, and Do-overs*

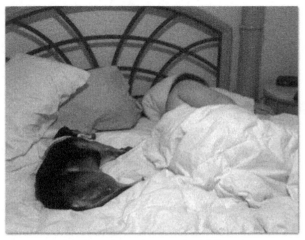

*Sometimes it's just a dog's life.*

Winter, 2003. One day my third wife, Mandy, brought home an unexpected gift: A small kitten. Mandy was searching for something to tear down the wall between us. She knew well my love of animals, and she hoped that drawing out my compassion for a vulnerable creature would help me share a little more of myself. My wife and I had known each other for more than four years, and we seemed to be moving farther apart every day, not closer together, and it was because I was lost in obsessive thoughts that I would never confess to her. Mandy didn't know exactly why I was so withdrawn and remote, but she was willing to try anything to get me to open up, to share a part of myself with another living thing.

I had always resisted having pets for one reason: They die. Ever since shooting that robin just to watch it die in the driveway, I'd been disproportionately affected by the suffering and mortality of other creatures. A dead squirrel in the road can ruin my day. A dead dog or cat can ruin my week. I had never experienced loss in my immediate family other than my grandparents, and I dreaded the inevitable moment when someone close to me died. I know I am not the only one who feels so deeply when it comes to animals, but sometimes I consider it a curse.

However, I was feeling no real compassion as my wife showed me the box with this three-month-old kitten in it—only irritation at this imposition of responsibility. At first, I was angry. "That is the most useless animal I have ever seen! Why didn't you ask me first?"

What Mandy said nearly broke my heart. "I know you have love in you. I've seen it. I want you to have something to love. Something that I hope can bring out what you seem afraid to show me."

Mandy was right. She was right about me being unable to open up to her, and she was right that caring for an animal would be an important step for me. With animals, there is no judgment. I was capable of showing animals an unconditional, sincere, open affection that I was too frightened to show the closest people in my life. I named the kitten "Useless," held her close to me, and cried.

May 18, 2004. Our marriage was on its last legs. Mandy agreed to come visit my shrink with me. It was unclear what I hoped to gain. I wasn't honest with my therapist or my wife, and there was no real hope of a breakthrough in our relationship. My shrink had no knowledge of my drug problems, eating disorders, and strange, obsessive-compulsive routines. Therapy built on a foundation of lies and denial. My wife had little more knowledge about my real problems than my shrink. I trusted no one.

There was lots of anger that day. "You won't show yourself to me! I want real intimacy!" Mandy railed. She was totally in the right. Mandy deserved my love That is marriage: Giving of yourself even in the face of self-doubt. I yearned to show that I could be intimate. To open up and reveal the man who wanted to be loved and had so much love to give. A man free of the constraints of a mind distorted by self-doubt. But I didn't know how.

Instead, confronted by my wife in the therapist's office, I did what I often did as a coping mechanism in stressful situations—I created an entire movie in my head about how things would go if I told the truth. The end of the movie was never positive. I will never share my real feelings, I thought. Too risky. I sat there mute as my wife begged me to open up.

My wife and I left that office no closer than when we had entered. I had given her no opening at any point in our exchange to share my deepest pain about my past and present. It was not much later that I took the path of least resistance that I had become so adept at to keep from opening myself up to anyone. I don't know how things would have gone if I had spoken the truth, but my lies led to inevitable results. A relationship pattern played out in all three marriages. I hope this book can, in some way, serve as a deeply deserved apology to all of my former wives.

I ran from my marriage with Mandy just has I had run from the others—back to where I felt more comfortable: Living a distorted life of lies and fantasies.

•

August 27, 2004. My cousin is getting married. I am flying out to Seattle Saturday morning on my brother's plane and then boarding a puddle-jumper to Orca Island for the wedding. It will be a happy day for my cousin and the entire extended Cuban family. Wheels up at 7 A.M.

One A.M. that morning. Still have an hour until last call. A group of cocaine buddies and I are closing down the local bar that doubles as a boutique hotel. It's one of my favorite places to party. The club has a "safe" bathroom—one that has stalls with solid closing doors. Addicts can never be too careful.

Now it's just before the 2 A.M. close. Have to get that last sniffy in. Back to the bathroom. No dollar bill. Left my keys on the table. Snorted it off the back of my hand. Ready to rock. More Jack and Diet Cokes! We go back to my place. Now it's 4 A.M. Incoherent jabber, watching *Scarface*. We recite our favorite line from the movie before each line of cocaine. "Say hello to my little friend!" We are one with *Scarface*. The thought that I have to be on a plane in a few hours vaguely penetrates the back of my cocaine brain. No sleep? No problem! A couple of black-market Xanax would do the trick, and, then, on the long flight to Seattle, I could sleep.

Just in time, I head to the airport, get on the plane—loaded with lots of close Cuban relatives—I pass out. The next thing I know it's wheels down in Seattle. I wake up with a raging Xanax, cocaine, and whiskey hangover, and I'm pissed off that I didn't bring a baggie of coke with me for a quick recovery. Still have to take the puddle-jumper to Orca. That will be fun! I'm determined not to puke in the puddle-jumper and thus announce my disrespect for my family, my cousin, her family, and last of all, myself. There's a minimum code of conduct for drug addicts. I survive the flight to Orca Island—barely. I'm in one of those tiny twin-engine planes that gets bumped around by every wind. I don't know how I keep from puking all over the plane. When we get to our rooms at the wedding site, I head straight to the toilet and upchuck. I am suddenly very uncomfortable being around so much family. Leaving my insular world of addicts and joining responsible, happy people who lead productive lives is always risky.

The wedding itself was unlike anything I had experienced before. It was set on a beautiful lake in the wilderness of Washington State. The sky over the green mountains was just a bit cloudy, and the air was alive with birdsong. The extended families of the bride and groom had come from around the world, and some folks were meeting for the first time.

I rarely looked anyone in the eye the entire trip. I was afraid they would see the addict within me, and I would sense their disappointment. I felt it regardless. Not because it was verbally expressed, but because I knew that my brothers knew. I knew they were disappointed in me. And I knew that my father didn't know; it would break his heart. I knew that my extended relatives did not know, save for my aunt, the mother of the bride. She was a clinical social worker, and I would sometimes reach out to her. Starting in 1990, after my first divorce, we would occasionally discuss my depression and feelings of unworthiness. But how could I possibly impose my misery on this joyful occasion?

During the wedding dinner, I was sitting at a long banquet table. One by one, family members stood up and toasted the bride and groom, and, the entire time, I stared directly at my plate of food. For some reason, fixating on a single point somewhere near my salmon and thinking about nothing but the plate gave me comfort and allowed me to listen to what was being said. If I looked at anyone, my mind would immediately start processing projected thoughts. Being able to focus on a fixed point and listen gave a normalcy to everything. No past, no future, only that moment. This would be my modus operandi for family events at the apex of my addiction.

As I watched my cousin being carried around in a chair to the song "Hava Nagila," a Jewish tradition, it occurred to me that the happier people were around me, the more miserable and depressed I became. I seemed to be in an almost hallucinatory state, even hearing little whispers: "Brian looks unhappy." "What's wrong with Brian?" I felt an urge to slip away into the Washington wilderness, never to be heard from again.

Really, I only wanted to get back to Dallas, to my safe haven of addiction and isolation. I wanted to be with other addicts and experience those increasingly rare moments when I could bask in the lie I had worked so hard to create. By 2004, drugs and alcohol offered less and less relief. And there was only raging depression when they didn't work their temporary magic.

When your entire world revolves around hanging with people who do nothing but get drunk and snort cocaine, such behavior seems normal when you stay within that world. To leave it is to risk having to deal with responsibility and accountability.

That can be a scary thought.

BDD wreaks heavy damage not just on physical health, but on relationships. Intimacy and honesty become impossible when you are unable or unwilling to share your true feelings about yourself with those who know you best. Throughout my life, I have repeatedly abandoned or destroyed any real chance of connection as soon as anyone gets close enough to sense my thoughts and feelings. As an adult, I needed to live in the moment to be happy. If I did not live in the moment, I had to re-live the past. And anyone who reminded me of my past felt like someone I had to stay away from. Gathered there on Orca Island was a whole embassy from my past, hundreds of friends and family who, in my mind, seemed poised to remind me of some horrifying or embarrassing moment, eager to laugh at me, happy to put me down. Of course, nobody felt anything but love and concern, but I couldn't have seen it that way at the time.

●

Fall, 2004. Single again. Craving love, another relationship. But it couldn't possibly be healthy. When relationships are entered into simply to fill emotional gaps, a need for validation, they can be as destructive as addiction.

It's 3 A.M. I'm standing at the top of the stairs, looking down onto the dance floor of a nightclub in downtown Dallas, watching my friends own the dance floor, moving with each other to the music, having a good time. I'm frozen in place on the stairwell. Someone, please come talk to me! My thoughts drift to the opening scene of *Bright Lights, Big City.* The movie opens with Michael J. Fox's character alone on a dance floor of a club, coked up and abandoned. Lonely. Wanting. I was that person. This was the only avenue I knew to find a relationship: Clubs, booze, and cocaine, with the occasional online dating service mixed in. The last drunk guy and girl in the bar. Do it all again tomorrow. It suddenly occurs to me: If I want to find a relationship, I need to change the scene. I need to feel like I'm the life of the party. If I'm too frozen to get out on the dance floor, I will bring the party to me. I will throw a party!

Invites go out. Mostly to women. Two hundred of my closest friends that I've never met! If I get enough of them in one place and provide the alcohol and the drugs, someone will notice me. I just want to be noticed without having to expose myself.

The party is on! Before the guests arrive, I strip naked in front of my bathroom mirror. I inspect every inch of my stomach, love handles, and back fat. I push it. I knead it. Do everything I can to experience the release of tension and shame before I head out into the crowd to try and meet my next wife. Then I dress and greet the early arrivals.

My favorite getting-wasted song, "Pump Up the

Volume," blasts out by the pool; there's a rented margarita machine, cocaine, and booze aplenty. As more people arrive, I alternate between entertaining my guests and doing drugs in my bedroom to capture that elusive golden moment of sociability.

Soon, I'm having a terrible cocaine trip. Sweating bullets in the unusually hot and muggy fall night. My stomach feels like it is bloating and expanding against my shorts. I keep lifting up my shirt to check it out. People are looking. I'm too messed up to care. I can feel my gut growing, like I am about to give birth to a creature from the movie *Alien*. The worse the buzz gets, the worse the expansion of my stomach feels. Everyone has to be able to see it now! The shame and self-consciousness is now more than I can bear. My heart rate has tripled. Getting dizzy. I think I'm having a heart attack. About to really take the party to another level by calling 911. Finally, I realize I'm having a panic attack.

I run back into the house and go up to my room. Calm down! Change to looser shorts. I try them all on until I find a pair that provides me mental relief. I grab a bottle of wine and chug most of the bottle, hoping the depressive effect will calm my heart rate. Go back out. I'm standing on the porch, dripping with sweat and reeking of cheap wine and cocaine breath. I'm watching people talk, drink, and dance by the pool, but I'm afraid to join my own party. I have nothing to say. I am once more standing on the steps, looking down at everyone having a good time. I am frozen in place. Is this really how I am going to meet my next wife? Back out to the crowd. I try to make small talk, but I'm mute in front of every woman I meet. Just asking if they are having a good time strikes fear in my heart. I think of the curly haired freshman at Penn State. Ugly! Ugly! I think of the sad rise and fall of each of my three marriages. You won't show yourself to me! What has changed? Nothing. I stagger through the crowd, just smiling and drinking while enduring the most irrational body-image fears I could conjure up. And my mouth . . . simply . . . won't . . . open . . .

It's now 5 AM. The last of the party stragglers are leaving. Once more, I am alone, cleaning up the mess of empty beer cans and used margarita cups. I have met no one. I have interacted with very few. How can I cope with this latest setback? The same way I have before. Out comes the frozen pizza. Add in a block of cheddar cheese left over from the party. Take it upstairs with a bottle of wine. Unlike at Penn State and Pitt Law, I live alone. No one but my pets to hear me retch as I release the pizza, the guilt of the calories, and the pain of the loneliness. The sound of birds chirping at 6 A.M. drives me nuts. It lets me know a whole night has passed, and I've neither slept nor had a good time. Time to pop a black-market Xanax and sleep the day away and send the party into the past.

Obviously, my cocaine-and-whiskey approach to dating was both dangerous and a terrible way to find a fulfilling relationship. The superficiality of the method—drugging myself for confidence and hoping someone would validate my ego by showing any interest in me—belied any chance of finding true love. However, it's a common mindset of people with self-image disorders. How I looked for relationships when I was single was reflective of how I lived in my committed relationships. It's not surprising that none of them lasted long.

The purpose of this chapter is not to outline every marriage disagreement and fight, because those are normal. There are, however, constants in how these relationships are affected by body dysmorphic disorder. Women who loved me never stood a chance, because I did not love myself—or even like myself, for that matter. Every romantic experience was just another shard of glass in a shattered mirror.

If you don't love or value yourself, you have only the wants and desires of your significant other to fill in the gaps of who you are. My mindset was entirely wrong, and it would remain that way until I came to understand the effect of a distorted self-image on my life. I'd spend so much time trying to understand how someone could possibly like me. Whenever conflicts arose, I'd wonder how far I could push my significant other before she finally admitted the truth (as I thought must be the case)—that she wasn't attracted to me, that she never had been, that I was ugly inside and out. Soon I'd become pissed off at a figment of my own imagination. Fights would ensue.

Sooner or later, anyone with any healthy sense of self-regard is going to get tired of it, even at the expense of love and marriage. You don't need to have a degree in counseling to know that is not a healthy relationship or one that will survive for the long term. That does not mean a relationship with a person with BDD cannot survive. It's all about overcoming the shame, and that's hard work. Is there anyone who has not experienced fear of rejection at one time or another? Imagine facing that fear every day, in the presence of the person you live with. There are so many barriers to recovery.

A common refrain in my failed relationships and marriages was my significant other telling me that I must think she was unattractive, because of my seeming unwillingness to be intimate with her both emotionally and physically. This, of course, led to a lot of strain in the relationships and, ultimately, was a large factor in their demise. When you're uncomfortable with your body and appearance, even if it is all imagined and exaggerated, intimacy can be a challenge. For me, libido was tied to how I viewed myself. If I felt good about myself, it was active; if I did not, it was depressed. A solid sense of self-worth—or at least a foundation for one—is key to the ability to share yourself mentally, emotionally, and physically with a partner.

And physical intimacy, of course, was just part of a larger problem. My lack of self-confidence led to a paralyzing fear of intimacy on any level. It's, frankly, something I still struggle with today, but, slowly, through counseling and forcing myself to open up—at first in safe surroundings and, then gradually, in public or in other, less-predictable environments—has helped me share myself and acknowledge the vulnerable boy I once was and face the man I am today.

The ability to tell that bullied child that he is safe and that everyone shares the same fears of rejection has been paramount in my recovery and learning to feel at ease around my loved ones. I actually have conversations with myself, imagining a one-on-one conversation with myself as a twelve- or thirteen-year-old. I do this often. I think back to different situations I have gone through and talk to that little boy, offering advice and perspective on life. We talk about weight. We talk about bullying. We talk about self-confidence. We talk about my mom. Of course, that little boy is long gone, and adults must deal with the real world in the present. The "conversations" however, have helped me gain adult perspective on what I experienced as a child. They have helped me let go of anger and sadness. They help me heal, little by little. The mirror that shattered so many years ago is, slowly but, surely, put back together, piece by piece. I still look, but now, I can process the reflection without the anger, without self-loathing. I have grown as a person, and I have grown in my relationships.

Better late than never.

# CHAPTER 7:
## *Pills, Booze, and a .45*

*My 40th birthday—making sure my nostrils were clear for a cocaine binge.*

*J*uly 22, 2005. A dark room. Table, desk, chairs. I'm with a staff psychiatrist of the Green Oaks Psychiatric Facility. I've heard of Green Oaks—it isn't far from my home in Dallas. Now, in the room with the psychiatrist, scenes of Jack Nicolson in *One Flew Over the Cuckoo's Nest* go through my muddled mind. I am in the middle of a crisis, and I'm thinking about movies. My brothers are sitting at the table across from me. As I sit and listen to the doctor's questions, I have a vague recollection of my younger brother rousing me from my bed and then having an angry confrontation. My .45 automatic had been lying on my nightstand. Then shock and confusion on the drive to the treatment center.

The residuals of cocaine, Xanax, and Jack Daniels are still coursing through my veins, but the fog is lifting slightly. Raging anger is settling in its place. Battle lines are being drawn in my mind. They want to take me prisoner. It's war. I'll lead the inmate rebellion.

Questions from the shrink pierce my anger like tracer rounds. What drugs have you taken? How are you feeling? Are you nuts! I'm angry! Do I want to hurt myself? Yes! Maybe! Not sure. Not sure of anything. The anger is too powerful. I believe if I died, it would teach everyone a lesson. My family. The kids who ripped my pants off. My mother. Myself, for being unable to fix the distorted reflection I see in the mirror each day. I can't tell him that! What answer will get me out of here? In the back of my mind, what's left of the internal lawyer takes over. I know that my family can't commit me, but he can. Proceed with caution. "If I wanted to hurt myself, there would have been bullets in the gun." I don't mention the fact that the person I had asked for bullets had ratted me out to my brothers. And I don't mention that I had been "practicing" sticking the barrel of the gun in my mouth and dry-firing the gun. I drift away, thinking about that night with the gun, the barrel in my mouth, my confused beagle, Peanut, watching from the doorway.

Ripped back to reality. Voices in the room. The doctor is talking to me again. When was the last time I used cocaine? I'm pretty sure it has been recently, since it was all over the room when my brother showed up. I had become the consummate liar in hiding the obvious cocaine habit from my family. It's that damn persistent cold that used to appear mysteriously every weekend. Now it's a daily occurrence. No one in this room is buying it.

Yelling. Accusations. All coming from me. I am angry at my brothers. I hate you! I want your attention! Now I have it! I am an eleven-year-old child, lashing out at my mother, who is a thousand miles away. They've taken away my control. What control? I'm out of control. Anyone in my line of sight is fair game. I'm blaming my brothers for everything that has gone wrong in my life. Why are they trying to hold me back? When I'm on drugs, I'm their equal. I can't even look at them. If I did, I would see nothing but love and concern. I look at the table. I look at my shoes. I find that fixed point on the floor that provides me comfort. I wish that shrink would stop asking me questions! The shrink is my enemy. My brothers have betrayed me. They're calm. Trying to make sure I am still above ground tomorrow.

I notice the room is not really dark. Sunlight pours through the windows, but I am in the darkest of places. I remember seeking a release of everything in me. Need those bullets! Too coked up and Xanaxed down to go out and buy some. Who do I know that can help?

More questions. Do I think I need help? Will I go to rehab? Sure, whatever will get me out of here! I lash out again. They have no right to do this. I yell across the table. "You have no right to control my life! I am an adult! Mind your own business!" They quietly let me rant. Letting me release the pain and loneliness of my reflection.

Blaming them for the darkness is so much easier than seeing the light. The doctor is asking calm, focused questions, to ascertain whether I am a danger to myself. At times, I am calm in my answers. At times, I am crying, angry at him and then at my brothers. Quit asking the same questions! I know your game! Quit treating me like an idiot!

So alone. More and more, I start to feel like the shy, introverted boy I once was. I'm no longer the sophisticated, in-shape, cover model I created in my imagination—the myth that drugs and alcohol and eating disorders and steroids and plastic surgery helped to forge.

Up until now, each day has been a battle to see someone different when I looked in the mirror. But, in this room, there is no reflection. I'm unshaven. Unkempt. I reek of booze and days of neglected hygiene. I'm as raw and vulnerable as I could possibly be. I'm exposed. And I can no longer escape the stark reality of how I was getting by day by day.

An hour has passed. The room is getting brighter. The love and calm of my brothers soothes me. Quiets me, softens my edges. It's always been there, but I wasn't present enough to sense it. I was thinking only of myself: My next high. My next drink. Without the drugs, what am I going to see in the mirror each morning? The thought terrifies me. My brothers calm me, and I begin to focus on my love for my family. Arms are around me. Holding me. I begin to feel the love penetrating my shell. They are not the enemy. There is a pinhole of real light, and it's beginning to expand. Should I go to rehab? What about twelve-step? I'm still on the defensive, but, at least for the moment, I can listen. Have to grab those moments. They don't come often.

After the one-hour psych evaluation, I was taken home from Green Oaks, wondering how I had brought myself to the brink of death so quickly. In reality, it was not quick. It was a gradual, lifelong descent, with just enough good moments to blind me to the reality of the slide. Even in addiction and body dysmorphia, there were good moments in my life.

It was decided that an out-of-state facility, away from my crowd of coke addicts and alcoholics, would be the most beneficial. But, ultimately, I would not go.

●

The journey that led me to Green Oaks was decades in the making, but the decision to go had been made just that very morning. Early on that summer day, I was roused out of a Xanax/alcohol/cocaine stupor by the sound of my younger brother's voice asking me if I was okay. He had used a key I had given him to enter my house. I had no memory of sending emails to my older brother hinting that I was going to kill myself. I don't remember emailing one of my close friends to obtain bullets for the Spanish Star Single Action .45 automatic he had given me as a gift a few years before. I have never been a fan of guns. But you don't have to be a fan to know what to do with one. I wanted those bullets. I was suddenly a gun person.

When my younger brother showed up at my house, there was an ample supply of cocaine, Xanax, and anabolic steroids lying around near a box of syringes, all set out in the open like props in a stage drama. I usually hid my illicit wares all over the house. I hid my cocaine in fake electrical outlets that I had installed in my walls, as if that was going to fool the cops or the drug dogs if my home was ever searched. The paranoia of an addict. But, that morning, I had no fear of carelessness, of being discovered. Maybe, this time, I wanted to be found out.

Then my brother spotted the gun on my nightstand, within my reach. Still unloaded, but he didn't know that. He asked me what I was going to do with the gun, and, then, he demanded it.

"Give it to me, Brian!"

I angrily pushed it in his direction. "Take it! It's not loaded." I wished it was. I wanted it to be. I was angry. Angry that he wanted my gun. Angry when he hinted he would confiscate my drugs, but too intoxicated to confront him. I passed out again.

Some time later, my older brother showed up. He had been out of town but flew home immediately. They made a call to an in-patient psychiatric facility in Florida that had a bed clear for me if I could get down there for screening. I did not push back, but I was angry at the prospect of leaving my home to go anywhere that was not my choice. The loss of control I had always agonized over when I looked in the mirror had become a stark reality, in the worst possible scenario. In the short term, they decided to take me to Green Oaks Psychiatric Facility. I didn't resist. I felt like I was at rock bottom. I was also still in a half-drugged haze of confusion. If a friend had come to my house instead of my brother, I probably would have pushed back and told him to leave me alone. But the shame of knowing my brother— who I loved with all my heart—had seen my situation was enough to get me to go.

As we left the house, my brother noticed the huge collection of bottles of alcohol in my bar, and the full scope of my problems started to become obvious. I was keeping the liquor store within walking distance from me in business. I had also gotten into the habit of chugging whiskey as a sleep aid if I had no Xanax or sleeping pills to bring me down from a cocaine high.

My brothers would take my supply, but I wasn't ready to be helped, so getting rid of the alcohol and drugs was a very short-term fix. It is virtually useless to take the alcohol from an alcoholic or the drugs from the drug addict, if they haven't surrendered to the need for help. It's only a delay until they can hit the liquor store again or call the dealer. It simply breeds resentment at the removal of independence and self-determination. Addicts can benefit from the right support, but only we can save ourselves. We are the only ones that can say "No."

As I slowly came out of my coke-and-Xanax stupor, we pulled into the Green Oaks parking lot. As my brothers spoke with the intake nurse, I filled out the intake form. The embarrassment and shame were overwhelming. I was a worthless stain on the Cuban name. I really did want to kill myself. Was this going to be in the next edition of the *Dallas Morning News*? The feeling was worse than when I stood on the side of the North Dallas tollway handcuffed in the DWI arrest back in 1991. At least then, I was only an embarrassment to myself. It was well before Mark's successes had made our family name well known in Dallas. Back then, I was just another drunk. My thoughts in the waiting room were of ego, not of recovery. On reflection, this was a red flag that there would be no recovery at that moment in my life.

In talking with my brothers on the drive home from Green Oaks, I strongly resisted the suggestion of rehab. As an alternative, they suggested that I confine myself to my house for a while and stay away from the Dallas party scene. To make the point, they took my car keys from me. I, frankly, should have been in detox and then rehab, but there was really nothing anyone could do if I was not ready to admit defeat.

Once home and without access to my car, I was angry all over again. I felt outrage at my family for trying to control my life as I defined it, so I took a cab to the auto dealership and bought a new set of keys. I was a good boy for a couple of weeks. I did not call my coke dealer. I did not drink. I'm cured, I thought.

But, sitting alone at home, I had nothing to think about except my old problems. Jeff had taken the gun, but my mind returned again and again to that night of "practice." Sticking the barrel as far back in my throat as I could and counting the seconds in my head from pressure on trigger to the click of the simulated firing. How many seconds to live. Click . . . Pull back the slide. One more time . . . Click . . . Just once more. I'm ready to release the pain . . .Click. The calm, warm, resigned feeling coursed from my stomach to my head when I played the game with the .45. Then I thought of my rescue dog, Peanut. Who will take care of her and my cat, Useless? Tears. I was bawling, and I noticed Peanut was at the door, watching. She was lying full length, with her head extended out, in her submissive position. Does she sense my pain? What is she thinking? Will she miss me? I will miss her. The thought of the only creatures on this earth that touched my soul and gave me unconditional acceptance caused me to consider the true meaning of what I was about to do. I hugged Peanut. I had no idea what would happen to me next.

Being home alone with just memories was excruciating. About two weeks after I had declared myself cured of cocaine, alcohol, and the club scene, I had had enough self-imposed isolation. Historical revisionism set in. I did not have a problem. I had simply gone through a bad time, I told myself. The solution was simple. I would not party during the week. I would use more cocaine and less alcohol to avoid chemical depression. If I could find the right balance for feeling good, everything would be okay. I would also be a responsible addict and always take cabs or have someone to drive me when I went out on the town. Problem solved.

By the time I was hauled off to Green Oaks, my career as a lawyer (to the extent that I had one) was hanging on by a thread. The fact that I hated what I did for a living made it so much easier to not care that the drugs, alcohol, and nightlife had pretty much substituted for any sense of pride in my work. My reputation in the community (to the extent that I had one) was destroyed. Everyone knew—they just didn't let on. Years later, as my recovery progressed, people would contact me and tell me about the ugly things I had said or done in the abyss of a cocaine personality. That inner-outer critic that bullied Hawaiian Dan and my father was on display every night.

•

September, 2005. Back out on to the Dallas party scene. At one of my favorite bars to get drunk and high with my usual party entourage. Sweating, shirt un-tucked to cover my gut (which really was a gut now, with all the weight I had recently gained). Staggering into the restroom, I don't notice that I have unzipped and exposed myself, fully out of my pants, before I even get to the bathroom. I stumble toward a stall. As I look down in a failed attempt to control where I'm peeing, I spot something. Holy shit! A large baggie filled with a white substance lies at my feet. Not your typical "hide it away" one-gram cocaine baggie. There's at least four or five grams of something in this huge bag. Could it be? Maybe? Have to pick that baby up! Zip it up! I spray my pants with my own piss as I quickly exit the stall. Suddenly, I have temporary amnesia regarding my recent near-suicide attempt and brush with involuntary commitment. I need to see if I have found what I think I have. The club is packed, so I can't find any cover to try it right there. I'm also paranoid that some drug dealer is looking for his stash. I need to get some privacy. Is this meth or blow? I don't do meth. I am a high-class addict.

High-tailing it out to my car in the parking lot.

It smells like coke. It has the consistency of coke. I am a cocaine connoisseur, being able distinguish the good shit from the stuff cut with too much baby laxative, B-12, methamphetamine, and other fillers. It's cocaine! Party time! Suicide and thoughts of rehab were a lifetime ago. I am happening again! At the top of the roller coaster, looking straight down.

I had no clue. It got worse after that. I was doing lines in the bathroom at work to pick me up from routinely getting in at the wee hours of the morning. The week, to me, was not about personal accomplishment or living a productive life. Each day was simply a set number of hours to struggle through. I started going to counseling sessions high on coke. "Honesty is the best policy" is not just a cute little saying in recovery. I was living one big lie. I lied to others about my behavior. I lied to myself about my physical and mental health. I even lied to my psychiatrist, who is supposed to be the one person I can truly let go with.

"How are you?"

"Fine, doctor."

"Are you using?"

"No, doctor."

"How are your anti-depressants working for you?"

"Fine, doctor."

Nothing that was said penetrated. My recovery could not even start without honesty. But here is the challenge: When you are in the throws of addiction, you may have no idea what "honesty" is. For me, honesty was whatever I told myself to rationalize my behavior. I wasn't looking to conquer addiction, eating disorders, and other potentially destructive behaviors. I only wanted to manage them. I will always have a driver. I will not party during the week. I will drink only certain types of alcohol. I will use diet aids or laxatives instead of engaging in bulimic behavior. I could always convince myself that I'd learned to manage my problems. I actually became a relatively high-functioning addict. The Brian I had once again created, however, would soon implode one more time. One last time.

•

January 15, 2006. Finishing up my week-long birthday party at the Candle Room, a popular bar in Dallas. One of my favorite hangouts. Not unusual for me to show up at 8 P.M. on a weekend and close it down, spending hundreds of dollars that I didn't have on booze, not to mention the curbside exchange for my $100 baggie of cocaine just off the Southern Methodist University campus. Six months after a gun in my mouth and a trip to the loony bin.

We were on the fourth day of celebration during my birthday week. Every night at a different club. A girl named Amanda came in with friends. She had been watching a Cowboys playoff game somewhere else and was invited by some people who were there to come by the bar. She caught me in that good thirty minutes when the cocaine and the alcohol made me that person I wanted to be. She was attractive, educated, and confident. We talked. We clicked. I had just met the girl who would eventually play a huge part in saving my life. We began to date. I, however, did not slow down.

April 8, 2007. I am in a daze. An hour before, I had been awakened by Amanda, who had just moved in two weeks before. She had been out of town visiting family for Easter weekend. I had no idea what day or time it was. There were alcohol bottles in the bedroom. There was a prophylactic on the bedroom floor by the bed. My black-market Ambien bottle was half empty. No idea how many I had taken. I went into denial mode. No woman had been there. Then I claimed there was a woman but that nothing had happened. But I didn't know for sure. I couldn't rely on my memory to supply me with any answers. Lies replaced lost memories all too easily.

Amanda wept. I denied everything. Here I was, again. This time, there was no gun. There were no brothers. But there was the person I wanted to spend my life with. And this was how I showed it. I was repeating the pattern, only, this time, with the most intimate of betrayals. As I slowly came out of my stupor, she pressed me for details of what had happened.

Between the frustration of not being able to remember and not being believed, I realized it. There was no control. There was no life. There was no future. I was naked in the mirror. I finally saw Brian. What I saw made me sick to my stomach. I had failed at life. In my mind, I had now failed every single person who had ever loved me.

I suggested we go to the Green Oaks treatment center. Not because I wanted to but because I had to do something to stave off her anger. I needed a buffer and time to reconstruct the events. The familiar forms. The familiar hour-long wait to see a doctor seemed like an eternity. Amanda next to me, distraught, angry, crying. As the hour ticked by, the frustration grew for both of us. We decided to leave. In the parking lot of the treatment center, I realized that, if I didn't get honest, starting at that moment, there would be no hope for our future or my future. It was time for the self-styled emperor to put away his fancy new duds. I had no idea what I'd do next, but, at least, having the rational thought was a start.

Why that thought at that time? Why not when I was chewing on the barrel of a gun six months earlier? I have no idea. How does an addict know that he or she may be looking into the abyss for the last time? You don't believe it when you hear it from someone else. I've given the lecture to others. Some listened, and some reacted as I had, with denial. Some are now dead by their own hand, intentionally or accidentally, by overdose. The hints that you party too much. Not showing up for work. Not leaving the house except to hit the bars. The roulette wheel of what you do after the bars close: live or die? Decide whether someone else lives or dies? There is no iPhone app or mathematical formula to let you know that the next line of coke may be your last or that the next drunk drive home may send an innocent family to their graves. These aren't typical things for an addict to think very hard about. If they were, there would be far fewer addicts.

I would no longer look into the abyss. I knew my family's love was unconditional, but I also knew they had limited tolerance for watching me destroy my life. They had families of their own. They had lives. Amanda was both angry and crying as we drove home. In my mind, it was over. She would be moving out and moving on with her life. Finding a healthy existence with a healthy partner. I was not that guy.

I however, did not want to lose the one thing that mattered most: The respect and love of those who had stood by me as I did everything in my power to destroy it. NO MORE! That was all there was to it. There was no miraculous cure during that drive. There was only the turmoil in my mind and a lost past and an unwritten future. I vowed to myself that, whether she left or stayed, whether my family rallied behind me or cut me loose, I would not take that step into the infinite darkness. I would search for the light.

The next day, I took a chance. It wasn't easy. I still had to confront the BDD issues: The unresolved bullying in my childhood and the resulting eating disorders, alcoholism, and drug addiction. I had not scratched the surface of any of it. The constant projection of negative thoughts had driven me into isolation. Trying to look that far into the future and grasp all of my faults was terrifying. But I wanted to live. I wanted to love, and I wanted to be deserving of love.

I finally saw myself as everyone else saw me. It was over. I would never step back, regardless of the pain.

Amanda and I returned to the house. She started to make preparations to move out and stay at a hotel that night. Then came the next conversation with family. I called both of my brothers. They were pragmatic. They had heard it before. I did not give them all the gory details. I simply stated that I had "slipped." An interesting choice of words that implied that I had—at any time—been "sober." Other than the three-week period after my brush with suicide, it had been business as usual.

Jeff is a former psychologist. We discussed rehab and the treatment options. He pushed for rehab. He had seen this before professionally. I resisted. I wanted to speak to the psychiatrist I had been seeing—and lying to, for years, about who I really was. There was a difference this time. I was ready to be honest.

April 9, 2007. I walked into my psychiatrist's office. After sharing the truth about what had really been going on in my life, my question for my doctor was simple. Did I need in-patient rehab? Detox? He responded with a blunt question. Of course, he knew about my prior brush with suicide. "Do you want to hurt yourself?" he asked.

Of course, I wanted to hurt myself! That's what I had been doing all along! Did I want to kill myself in the sense of using that .45 automatic my brother confiscated? No, I didn't. Like then, I wanted the pain to go away. Like then, I was prepared to go to great lengths to do it. Now, however, I was ready to move above the beam, not below it.

"No," I told the psychiatrist. I did not want to end my life. I wanted to have a life. A real life of looking forward to each day, not surviving it. A real life of seeing a human being in the mirror every morning, not a monster. Seeing Brian, as an imperfect and flawed creature—like everyone else—without it sending me back into that spiral of unhealthy behaviors. I needed to add some healthy, healing behaviors to the rotation.

It isn't always clear how we get to the point where we're open to changing our lives. For many, it comes of tragedy. For some, the bar is not so low. It may just be shame. Being tired of hurting others. Tired of hurting yourself. For some, it does not happen at all.

My ultimate low point did not involve anything that could not be rebuilt over the years. My self-esteem. My view of my body. My thought process of how others perceive me. The trust of my loved ones. In addiction recovery, it's sometimes said that your lowest moment is your best if you survive it and learn from it. Hopefully, you have not hurt yourself or anyone else irreparably before you reach that point.

*Amanda and Brian.*

# CHAPTER 8:
## *Step by Step, Year by Year*

*A*pril 10, 2007. I walk up to the door of the building where the local twelve-step meetings are
held. My shrink feels that a trip here is the first step
to recovery. If this doesn't hold, then I'll have to go
to rehab. Lucky for me, the twelve-step building is
right next to my shrink's office. If it hadn't been convenient, I might have just made excuses to not go at
all. For an addict, excuses are often more plentiful
than reasons for recovery. The present is more important than the future—the present of the high.

This morning, however, there's a difference. I
do not see a fat, stupid child when I first look in the
mirror. I see an aging, defeated adult. A man defeated
by years of eating disorders and drug addiction. Defeated by a life of quick fixes and miracle cures that
did more harm than good. I'm frightened of what I
see—but not in the usual way. Now, my fear is that
the person in the mirror is about to lose everything
he loves. I was always so happy in my isolation, but,
in this moment, I realize what it would mean to be
truly without love, trust, and hope. I have to find a
way to become more than the sum of my obsessive
thoughts. I have to get into honest, focused treatment. If fear is my motivator, I'll take it.

After pacing around outside the twelve-step
building for a long time, I finally peer in the door,

down the long hallway, to where people are gathering. I'm afraid of being recognized. My ego is still paramount in my worries. I'm ready for change but not ready to give up my pride.

I pace outside the door of the building for another ten minutes, sometimes opening the door a bit, but never going in. For a time, I sit listlessly in a nearby sandwich shop.

When I finally work up the courage to walk into the building, each step into the unknown seems harder and harder. Who are the people I'll meet in twelve-step? My mind flashes back to one of my favorite childhood movies, *Willy Wonka & the Chocolate Factory*. I suddenly imagine that, as soon as I enter the twelve-step meeting room, I'll be carried away by a team of chanting Oompa Loompas determined to punish me for my bad habits. I have no desire to meet the Oompa Loompas on the other side of that door. I again consider rehab. But I'm even more embarrassed about the idea of my friends and everyone who knew my family name finding out I'd be going to in-patient rehab than I was about a small group of strangers scrutinizing my deepest flaws.

I finally make it to the door of the meeting room, and I can smell the fumes of stale cigarette smoke and day-old coffee. My eyes lock onto the 1950s tile floor, ingrained with the dirt of countless feet. There are other people milling around in the hall. Are these the people with whom I was supposed to share my darkest secrets? Would I be made fun of, teased, bullied, insulted? Who are these people? Skid-row bums? That's my perception of twelve-step. I think of Nick Cage's character, Ben, living in the sleazy "no-tell motel" as he drinks himself to death in *Leaving Las Vegas*. Dick Van Dyke's character, Charlie, drunk, alone on the beach, with no future in *The Morning After*.

I'm still not ready. I don't go in. I walk back to my car, and I sit there with the key in the ignition. I even start the engine. But I don't go anywhere. Instead, I think about my next move. It's all on me. I could drive on home and check out my bathroom mirror. Go through all my routines. I might get through the next day, and the next. But any comfort would be temporary. I would certainly restart the cycle of destruction. My shrink couldn't save me. Therapists can only do good work if their patients are honest, a quality rarely found among addicts or sufferers of BDD. This is the biggest decision I've faced yet.

As I sit, paralyzed, in my car, I think of another recurring dream. The dream begins as I walk out the door of my house. I have no girlfriend or wife, no friends, no family. No one who loves me. I feel hollow and empty, like I'm experiencing a kind of starvation. I start walking. I feel I have to begin a new journey. Somewhere. Anywhere. But I can't walk past my driveway. My legs just won't carry me—it's like I'm in quicksand. So I grab my bike, the one my father bought me as a child, but the tires are flat. I manage to get the bike to a bike store, and they replace both tires. But those are also flat. As I leave the bike store, I try walking again, but now the sidewalks are icy and slippery—I can barely move. But I must go. I must go somewhere far away. Northern Canada seems a good destination. I need to walk until I reach a place of total isolation. To be away from everyone who knows me, who can see through me. I know leaving will hurt my family. I want them to see how much I hurt. I'll run away. I'll show them. I keep walking. Now my feet are moving as fast as I can lift them, but I am going nowhere. I am completely stuck in place.

I shut off the engine and take the keys out of the ignition. There's no way to escape my problems. I have to face them. I go back to the front door of the meeting room. Deep breath. Don't look around. Eyes down at the floor. That fixed point. Watch the feet move forward. One baby step at a time. It's the way I'm able to accomplish things in life. It's how I was able to finish eight marathons. Facing any difficult task, my best self is that part of me that can place one foot in front of the other until a goal is accomplished. Don't look left. Don't look right. Don't think about the finish line. Watch your feet, one in front of the other. Again. One in front of the other, back down the long hallway. Now, open the glass door. People are looking at you. Don't look at them! Fixed point! Open it!

I do. And I go in.

●

I am not here to advocate twelve-step. I think everyone with addiction problems, BDD, or other psychological roadblocks needs to find their own treatment programs with the help of professional treatment providers. While the basics of addiction or BDD may be similar for everyone, we are all unique in our needs. What's more, not every person with BDD has the same issues. I had both BDD and addiction to work through, and first I had to gain control of the addiction behaviors that could kill me. What twelve-step did for me was provide structure early in my recovery. I believe that, whatever the treatment mode, structure is important. Living in chaos, hoping I could fix my life all on my own, simply did not work for me. One of the most important assets twelve-step gave me was the realization that I was not going to be able to do it on my own. I had already failed at that.

At some point, addicts and BDD sufferers have to take that all-important step and talk about their true feelings with people they can trust. A twelve-step program can offer that. Getting honest in treatment sessions helped as well. Family was another option for me. Maybe you don't have that kind of family support system. Maybe it will be a friend. Maybe it will be rehab. Find someone who will listen. Was there fear of judgment when I first started telling my story to others? Yes, but I quickly found there was no judgment. No disgust. It slowly became easier to reveal my true self in both self-help group treatment and in one-on-one therapy. There are options available for everyone. The upside is a happy, productive life.

As I got more and more sobriety under my belt and my mind cleared, I was able to at least begin to envision how to restore order in my life. I was also able to prepare myself for the hardest test of all—confronting the past. I couldn't do that in a twelve-step room; it was the wrong tool. Other resources gave me the opportunity and encouragement to get real about my past, without fear or deep depression. Intensive counseling and medication would help make facing my past possible.

April 11, 2007. Amanda has moved out and is living in a hotel. I'm by myself now, taking the first ceremonial acts of the recovering addict. First, there's the need to sanitize the house of all the paraphernalia of pain and addiction. It takes only a few minutes to fill a heap of garbage bags with bottles of alcohol. Even all the crystal glassware has to go. Thousands of dollars' worth crashes into the dumpster, shattering like the false reflection in the mirror.

Wine bottles customized with my name are next into the garbage bin. The sweet, fermenting smell of old booze bottles and moldy, withered limes mixes with stale pizza and soured milk in the dumpster.

Then, an unexpected find! A baggie of cocaine left from God knows when and by God knows whom. There were so many drug users going in and out of my house, it could have been anyone. It could have been me who left it around. I don't remember. After having slipped back into the cycle of Xanax, cocaine, and booze that almost ended my life, memories of any one specific party are hazy.

What to do? My nostrils sense that familiar cocaine smell. Neurons fire. Nose twitches. There's a dollar bill in my pocket; it would be so easy to roll. Pause. Fear. I can't hurt my Amanda again. I can't hurt my family. And finally, I cannot tell one more lie. It's time. Even in the first days of recovery, I'm able to grasp that vague hope of a future devoid of all the unhealthy and destructive behaviors of my past. Just a thought in the back of my mind, flickering like a candle that the weakest breeze could extinguish. But it's there. I have to go forward. Release, drop, and flush. I watch as the last cocaine I would ever touch circles down the toilet.

I sit down on my bed, relieved at what I've done, but already afraid of the next test. Maybe next time I would not flush it, or, huddled over the toilet, I'd revert to bulimia. Fear of failure is primal. Everyone goes through it at some point in his or her life. It can take us to the lowest lows or drive us to great achievement and feats of courage. I had been afraid my entire life. Afraid of my mother. Afraid of girls. Afraid of being alone. Afraid of the programmed responses in my head.

But sometimes we find courage even in fear. The courage to take that first small step and, then, to take another. As I lay in bed the night after my first twelve-step meeting, I am the same person I was the day before. I still have fear. After all, my life as I know it is over. I don't know what will come next. Would Amanda stay by my side after her greatest humiliation? Would I end up on the street living under a bridge, as nameless as I had dreamed of being, with no one who loved me? Would I be above ground in a month, a week, the next day? These thoughts raced through my mind as I fell asleep.

Dreaming of Atlantic City. I am four years old. Standing in the water. Looking for my parents. My earliest memory of life. Lost, crying, afraid. The water keeps getting deeper, pulling me out to sea. I am screaming. Mommy! Daddy! Where did they go? They were just sitting there, and, now, everything is different! I don't know where I am. Pulled further out to sea. I see them! Help me! They can't hear me. Water enters my lungs. Flailing. Screaming. Drowning.

I wake early in the morning, listening to the songs of the robins outside. I used to hate their songs. They made me sick to my stomach. Reminders of my act of cruelty so many years ago. Reminders of being on all-night coke binges, of self-loathing after being up for two days straight. But, this morning, the sound is different. The robins' song sounds like a call to courage. A reminder to try to reach out, day after day, step after step, to listen to others, and to make sure I was being heard, too.

The next evening, I call the person I'd been ashamed to reach out to. I call my father. My father is closest to my true heart. In many ways, my father is me. I confess everything to my dad, and we make a plan. I can't stay in my empty house full of terrible memories. I move in with him. Every day, I return to my home to take care of and spend time with my beagle Peanut and my cat Useless. But I spend every night with my dad. Every night we talk. Every night I feel safer. Those talks that I ached for as a child but was too afraid to ask for.

Moving day. Amanda and I had been living together only about a month before I wrecked things. She had to fly out of town the day after our tearful confrontation, so I had not spoken to her much since then. Moving day would make addressing my fears unavoidable. I'd have to look her in the eye and face my betrayal while helping her move into what I thought would be her own future—without me.

My thoughts drifted back to Memorial Day, 2004. Same scenario but with my ex-wife Mandy moving out. Then, I had no desire to aid in the process. I was not ready to face my failure. But this time, I had to. I had to look Amanda in the eye. It was hard. Every BDD-projected thought I could muster was going through my head. I could hear her thoughts of disgust. In reality, very few words were spoken as we moved her into her new place. I wanted to talk nonstop and convince her of my willingness to change with bullshit words. I resisted. I knew I would have to show her with actions, if she gave me that opportunity. I wanted the day to end. The process of moving every piece of furniture, every book, every lamp, seemed to stretch on endlessly.

But, sometimes, you just have to face the fire when you know you may get burned. By helping her move, I had effectively chosen to walk into the bonfire, and, lucky for me, I recognized it. If I had taken the path of least resistance and parked my ass on the couch, feeling sorry for myself, I would have lost her forever. I reminded myself of that with every cardboard box I hauled to the moving truck.

Visit number two with my shrink, after rock bottom. I have three twelve-step meetings under my belt. I have told him about the cocaine, booze, and failure to manage my medication. I was still not ready to reveal my most shameful secrets: The fat kid. The bullied kid. The eating disorders. My mother. My view of my own body. My fear of what others thought of me. Where do I start? How do you dismantle problems that took forty-plus years to construct? It was so daunting that fears of helplessness and relapse spun through my mind. But I had to find some way to reveal myself.

Then my therapist asked the question that would set me on a new course. "Brian, do you remember your dreams?"

My dreams. My vivid, colorful, movie-like dreams. I had a gift for remembering them clearly, even days later. "Yes, I remember them…"

I dream of law school often. Of finding out years later that I didn't have enough credits to graduate and my law degree had been taken away. Dreams of being unable to find my locker in high school. Dreams of my failed relationships. I tell my therapist about one in which I visit my gym. I arrive, and there's nothing but mirrors. What happened to the equipment? I have to get out of here! Where did my clothes go! I'm naked! Running to the locker room. More mirrors. No lockers. Look down at a fixed point by your feet. But there are mirrors on the floor. Where are my clothes! Why am I naked? My mouth is open, trying to scream. Nothing comes out. I am frozen in place. Eyes glued shut, don't want to see my reflection. The ugly nakedness of my existence. "What about dreams of childhood, Brian?"

I become uncomfortable and silent. Those are

the dreams about my deepest shame. Dreams from which I'd wake crying and screaming. Dreams of being pantsed. Dreams of being that fat, shy boy.

"Yes," I finally admit, "I have dreams about that." They were my most heavily cloaked secrets—stories I nursed that would allow me to relive my pain and maintain my anger at the past. I did not want to talk about them because I did not want to let go of the anger. I did not want to forgive anyone, let alone myself.

"Why don't you want to talk about those dreams, Brian?"

"They're too painful."

"Well, yes, that's why you're here. To confront that pain in a safe environment."

"How do I know it's safe? My mind tells me it's dangerous."

"Take a chance here, Brian. Tell me just one."

I start to cry. I start sobbing. The release of years of repressed emotion wracking my body. Memories of children tearing at my clothes resurface. I hated those kids. For the first time, I relive my pain out loud. One small step into the past and one giant step toward recovery.

After two weeks of living with my dad, I was ready to go back home. Back home to begin the process of repairing the relationship with the woman I loved. Back home to move full speed ahead to the next stage of my journey. Back home to the pets that I loved more than myself. I also went home with something I could not recall experiencing in many years—I went back home with hope.

Back with my therapist. Counseling shifted from lies and cocaine to talk of childhood. Talk of a strained and sometimes volatile relationship with my mom and my stories of bullying and isolation. Stories that I was too scared to ever bring to the forefront of my consciousness. With each story of bullying, loneliness, and rejection, there were a lot of tears. The process of picking apart my ego with my shrink was detailed and agonizing. I was invoking my past and facing much of it in a rational (though often emotional) way for the first time. That is not to say all my memories were awful, but the negative aspects were sometimes all I could remember. There is a saying that our memories are simply "memories of memories." The mind plays a lot of tricks, filling in gaps and fabricating details. Much like the documented unreliability of eyewitness testimony in court, our eyewitness "testimony" about our past can be faulty.

The first year of recovery was hard. I was unsure of who I was supposed to be and who I actually was. Cokehead Brian? The little fat boy in the mirror? Who was Brian? I often wept—in treatment *and* in my dreams. Agonizing, gut-deep wailing as I released all the fear and self-loathing of a shy little boy. Role-playing helped me get through it. I'd talk to younger versions of myself. I told him that it was okay to be who he was. He didn't believe me. At first, I didn't believe it myself.

During role-play, I often looked at photos of myself from that time period. I would tell my younger self there would be tough times. I told him that he is loved. I told him that his mother loves him but is lost in her own abyss. I visualized our conversation like a full-length movie in my mind. I played out all the younger versions of my family, alternate outcomes of my life. It was not an easy game to play. In fact, it's the flipside of the dark, obsessive thoughts of past humiliations that helped define and drive my BDD for so many decades.

In the past, I might relive episodes of pantsing or summer-camp misery again and again compulsively, always sinking deeper and deeper into depression. I've found the most positive way to combat those obsessive memories is to play with them, flip them upside down, retell them to myself with vastly different outcomes. These days, I role-play a satisfying response to the girls who rejected and ridiculed me because of my weight. I sing "Let It Be" in that talent contest just like the original Beatles. Role-playing can release a lot of emotion. I did some in structured therapy and some at home by myself, playing all the characters. Anyone who thinks this is something that might be beneficial for them should check with their treatment provider first.

•

2008. I had still not told anyone about my battle with eating disorders. While I still had thoughts, sometimes overwhelming, I had not engaged in any bulimic or anorexic behavior since I had gotten sober. I was engaging in numerous BDD tic behaviors but had no idea there was a diagnosis for it. Twelve-step was very useful in conquering the feelings that had led to eating disorders, even though my program was not designed to directly address behaviors aside from substance abuse. Talking about my problems in a group setting helped me get past my tension in a healthy way. I was also starting to understand that all my problems might be related, from addiction to my eating habits. But I had no concept that in-patient treatment had become available specifically for eating-disorder treatment. Seem silly for an educated guy? Not really, because, even after I stopped engaging in bulimic behavior, I still had not acknowledged that I had an eating disorder. It was just part of my life, like breathing and basketball. Then there was the shame. The all-consuming disdain for something that I thought only women experienced. As a male, I felt totally alone. Was I alone? An aberration?

May 19, 2008. I was scanning the Internet for news. A daily routine for me. Playing on Facebook. Ranting on Twitter. Finding outlets of expression and emotional release. I came across an article about the model Anna Caroline Reston, who died at the age of twenty-one from multiple organ failure secondary to anorexia nervosa. Anna weighed 88 pounds at the time of her death. I started doing more research, coming across story after story about struggles with eating disorders.

There was one constant: They were almost all written by women and about women. While I felt alone, the pure statistics told me I wasn't—I read that men often suffered from eating disorders as well. But where were these men? Were they all as ashamed as I was? Afraid to break the stereotypes of eating disorders being a female problem? I had already begun blogging and writing expressively as a form of therapy. No one told me it worked, but I knew it did, because it allowed me to pour raw emotion into the written word without fear of the response. I never feared being judged for my words, only for my looks. Public expression online was easy for me.

So I wrote. I told my story. That May day in 2008, I let the Internet know that I was Brian Cuban and that I was a recovering anorexic and bulimic. No one laughed. No one ridiculed me. The feeling of relief and power to change the course of my life left me exultant. I did not need to binge and purge. I did not need to do cocaine. I needed to write. My recovery arsenal had grown. I now had twelve-step, my family, therapy, and expressive-writing therapy. All of these tools contributed to repairing the shattered mirror.

As part of my recovery, I had to come to an understanding of what BDD is, that I had actually had a disorder with a name, and that I could make the choice to do something about it. Then I had to commit to doing things outside of therapy in my day-to-day life to address the behaviors.

Of course, my BDD is not gone. It probably never will be. Will I catch myself looking at my reflection in a window as I walk down the street? It doesn't happen as much as it used to, but it still does. Will I linger in front of the bathroom mirror now and then, staring at my love handles? Sure. How do I deal with all these little behaviors that some may view as eccentric or narcissistic but that I know are the by-products of an OCD-related affliction with BDD? Recovery is not an all-or-nothing proposition. It is a process. Your process may not be the same as mine. We are all unique, beautiful individuals, with our own, singular, life experiences.

Once I had an understanding of BDD, I began utilizing incremental cognitive behavior therapy (CBT) to deal with the mirror. It's an accepted method for dealing with body dysmorphic disorder. Most people with BDD can understand the uncomfortable love/hate relationship with mirrors. It is the tic that I have worked the hardest to get over. A basic example is that I spend excessive amounts of time staring at myself in the bathroom mirror. Am I admiring my "beauty" in a narcissistic way? No, I am fixated on what my mind still often tells me is my ugliness.

Incremental cognitive therapy has helped me change the way I behave after seeing myself in the mirror. One morning, I may approach the bathroom mirror and think, "I look awful!" Another morning I may think, "I can't go out today because I look so bad." I can generally fight through that, but the thought itself adds a component of increased depression, which can affect the way I function throughout the day. Cognitive behavior therapy has helped me realize that I am not the same as my negative thoughts. It's a slow, incremental, but beneficial process that should be discussed with a treatment professional.

Medication also played a crucial role. Certain types of antidepressants are known to be effective in treating OCD. As of the writing of this book, I am on 20 mg of Lexapro a day. I have taken as much as 40 mg a day. It has substantially lowered my obsessive-compulsive desires related to my BDD tics. When lowered, it is easier to address them with CBT. These are all matters you should consult a therapist about. As an example, using medication and CBT, I have been able to successfully eliminate most of my shower inspection tics. The shower-inspection was not ruining my life other than running up my water bill—but, as a non-life-altering tic, it was a good place to start and get comfortable with the therapy. Then I moved onto the ones that *were* life-changing, such as the mirror revulsion/fixation. To enjoy life, you have to be able to go out into public and experience social uncertainty. I was eventually ready to challenge the thoughts that drove me to social anxiety and isolation.

As the first two years of sobriety passed, positive thoughts about myself became more frequent. There were also thoughts of drugs and alcohol—but not in the sense of a physical need to partake. I'd still have the impulse to purge every time I passed a restroom with a full stomach. I still dreamt up ways to control my body, to transform my looks. But I was learning to master the triggers that set the thoughts in motion. For me, recovery came about by taking these important steps that I think might apply to many sufferers of BDD.

First, for any addict or individual suffering from destructive compulsive behavior, the first challenge is getting the behavior under control. It's hard to do that without outside support, which was why a twelve-step program was essential in my recovery. Rehab may work for some, and others may find their own support systems. But controlling damaging behavior is hard to do without support.

Another breakthrough that changed my life and made recovery possible was getting honest. Both with myself and others. Only when I had no choice but to face reality—that I had hurt my loved ones deeply and that I was bound for self-destruction— was honesty an unavoidable possibility. It's not enough to simply have an honest moment, however. Recovery requires a constant, conscious effort to be honest with yourself and share feelings with those you trust, both professionals and loved ones.

Which brings me to another pair of key break-throughs for me: Finding a safe place and a safe person. For me, twelve-step was an initial safe place to get addiction under control, and the people there had made a commitment not to judge each other. More than this, though, the two weeks I spent living with my father, confiding in him, discussing my life, and feeling his love and support were critical in finally turning my life around for good. Later, Amanda became a trusted partner again, as did the rest of my family. For addicts in the middle of crisis, ready to change, it's so important to find a safe place, free from stress triggers, and to connect with those people closest to youm whom you trust the most. I knew that, eventually, I had to face a world full of triggers and still keep an even keel, but big risks can start with small, safe beginnings.

As I learned from the first couple years of so-briety, simply avoiding negative behaviors is not enough. True healing can only occur when compul-sive negative thoughts are replaced with positive ones, and the only way to do that is to take negative thoughts head on. To truly get better, I needed to confront the past. Only since I figured out how to play with memory, reliving bad experiences with an attitude of love and acceptance, have I been able to free myself from impulses guided by embarrassing and depressing memories.

Forgiveness—for those who had hurt me, for myself for hurting others—extended naturally out of confronting the past. My reconciliation with my mother has helped immensely in turning my life around, and understanding her challenges has given me wisdom about my own. Letting go of anger has allowed me to embrace the positive aspects of my life again.

Finally, I was able to go from mere survival to real joy only when I learned to embrace fear and take positive risks. I understand my challenges now, and I've learned to live with them and even love them. From dancing with the stars (you'll see!) to simply engaging strangers in polite conversation on the elevator, I know that managing my dysmorphic thoughts is a constant challenge—and a challenge that I can meet playfully through small goals I set for myself every day.

●

June 16, 2008. I walked out onto the stage in

front of almost one thousand people. I was thinking back to that day at the camp talent show. A disaster then from not only a talent standpoint but also from a self-image standpoint. In 1971, I could only croak. At 47, I was no less scared than I was at ten.

This time around, I wasn't performing to turn myself into a rock star. I was challenging myself

*Testing my thoughts and taking risks.*

to reach out, expose my vulnerabilities, and think about how my actions might help others. This local Dancing With the Stars contest benefitted an animal charity. My love of animals sometimes exceeds my love of people, which was why I said "Yes" to something I knew would be extremely difficult. I prepared. They offered eight free dance lessons with the commitment. I paid for many more. I hadn't felt so driven to prove that I had control over my body and my future since I first began to starve myself. Since I first put my finger down my throat. This time, however, I had chosen to gain that feeling of control through a different behavior—a positive behavior.

My partner and I began to dance. It was a West coast swing number, the Brian Setzer Orchestra belting out "Put Your Cat Clothes On." I was sweating profusely under my blue-striped gangster suit and black-and-white winged-tip shoes. I was scared—of what people thought of my dancing, of failing. Most of all, I was terrified that all the people in the audience were scrutinizing every defect of my face and body, just as I did every morning. The thoughts were there. I wanted to un-tuck my sweat-drenched shirt so it would hang loosely over my stomach. I resisted the urge. I found a fixed point: my dance partner. The crowd and its imagined criticism disappeared.

One foot lands in front of the other. One movement flows into the next. Savor the moment of beating back the fears that I had lived with for a lifetime. The music stopped. I grabbed my dance partner's hand. Bowed to the audience. I did it! I had tested my worst fears and false thoughts, and emerged triumphant. I laughed into the shattered mirror. The audience applauded. I had done it. I had taken another step towards living a BDD-free life. I had forced myself into the breach of judgment and found none—only support.

I began to realize that this was the way the world worked. There are no mirrors that judge you. There are real people who see the real you, or they don't. When I finished the dance and the judges sent in their scores, I was not the best dancer, but the emotional victory was almost more than I could handle. I looked out into the audience for my Amanda and the friends who were all holding signs they had made to support me. Real signals of love and respect. I remember telling myself standing there on the stage that I wanted to remember that feeling of knowing that it's okay to be afraid. I smiled out into the crowed and waved. It's all good.

I kept setting new challenges for myself. Winter, 2009. Brian goes to Hollywood! Well, not really, but it was time to test those limits again. Not as drastic as joining the Marines, but I decided I'd put myself out there for hundreds of thousands of people to see, even if just for a few seconds, as an extra on a TV show. When I was approached, my first thought was, "Not a chance in hell." I don't enjoy walking around in public—I had no interest in letting potentially millions judge my fatness and baldness on the small screen. But I thought back to that stage and the West coast swing. I had taken a huge step in re-programming my brain. I could not go back. I had to take a deep breath, lengthen the stride of the next step, and move forward. I took a bit part in a television series that was being shot in Dallas. I had no desire to get into the acting business. I wanted to put myself in a situation where I knew negative thoughts might arise. I could then challenge them with facts—a more advanced version of challenging my thoughts when I looked in the mirror.

I would play a UPS delivery person. In the scene, I stood in an elevator with the actor Billy Zane. Being on a set as an extra is sort of disorienting—there's so much happening that you don't know who is paying attention to you or when you're in the shot. To me, it didn't matter. It wasn't about being noticed. It wasn't about being on television. It was about facing my fears of being ugly, shy, and not good enough. It was like standing onstage and looking into the biggest mirror in the world.

The episode airs! I refuse to watch it. I can't look at myself. I'm not as okay as I thought I was. I record the episode. I let it sit. What am I afraid of? It's silly. None of the other viewers probably even noticed the guy who was onscreen for two seconds. Eventually, I make myself do it. Turn on the tube. Hit play. I can't look, I just squint through one partially open eye. Shit! I missed my part. Rewind, force both eyes to stay open. There I am! I laugh. I look goofy in the scene. Who cares? It's just Brian. He's an adult, and he doesn't need to worry about what others think. I can see myself smiling on the elevator. A smile was not in the script. It was a smile of letting go.

•

Of course, recovery wasn't easy, and it didn't always mean moving forward. Summer, 2010. Setbacks suck. I lie in bed, weeping uncontrollably, in a deep depression. I'm sleeping a lot. I don't want to leave my house. I've suddenly become fixated on all the years of my life I've wasted. On all the pain I've caused my family. I have lost focus. It happens. A function of obsessive-compulsive disorder.

In to see my shrink. I'm still crying, so depressed I can't think straight. It's the most dangerous time if left untreated. So many deadly and destructive paths to be taken. Some I have been down, some I have not even thought of yet.

"Has anything changed?"

"I don't think so. I just can't stop thinking about the wasteland I've left behind me and the time I'll never get back, absent a change in the theory of relativity."

"Why aren't you focused on the progress you've made and your bright future?" he asks. The question makes me suddenly angry.

"If I knew that, I wouldn't need you."

"Do we need to increase your meds? How are you doing with those?"

"Well, I haven't been taking them. I was feeling good."

"Sounds like part of the problem to me. What do you think?"

Duh!

Finding the right balance of the right medication is not a standardized process. I know, from experience and from watching others, that the trial and error can be enough to cause a person to stop. I had been on and off anti-depressants dating back to my second marriage. Unfortunately, none of my short-lived and sporadic attempts at therapy during those times had any focus beyond controlling the grief of loss and failure. I had no knowledge of the role of certain types of anti-depressants in relieving the symptoms of the obsessive-compulsive behavior that often goes hand in hand with BDD.

•

I've had other setbacks and other challenges. A key realization for me is that I'll never be "cured," that every day will be a challenge, and that I need to embrace those challenges.

June 12, 2011. The Dallas Mavericks are the NBA champs! Their first title ever, and I could not be happier for my older brother, Mark, who owns the team. I wasn't a basketball fan growing up, but I am a fan of my brothers. I was immensely proud to see Mark get this much-earned reward after eleven years of hard work and some near misses. I went to Miami, Florida, for the finals.

I was no stranger to Miami, particularly South

*The Cuban men celebrating a Dallas Mavericks Championship.*

Beach. At the apex of my destructive behaviors, I was visiting South Beach regularly. I did not visit to hit the beach. I did not visit for the great food. I visited regularly because cocaine was in high supply, and I could get as messed up as I wanted without being noticed by anyone who might know me. I was also incredibly jacked up on steroids when I was going regularly.

I would hit South Beach, call my dealer, and go to the clubs. I would start comparing myself to every guy there. I would focus on their stomachs and the good-looking girls they were with: I had to be like that. I had to do more steroids! I had to work out harder! I needed more coke, or I would never be like that! I would be that fat kid told by his baseball coach to pretend he was chasing a refrigerator. I could even hear the girls saying it to me. Why the hell would I be interested in you? Go chase a refrigerator. That's what you're good at. The shame and self-consciousness would build up to an unbearable level. The only way to deal with it was more cocaine. I would look at different people in the club and create entire scenarios of them telling me I was fat and ugly. Then I'd get angry and leave. I'd go back to where I was staying and do more drugs. Then pop a Xanax to pass out. I repeated this cycle every time I went to South Beach. After I left, I'd tell myself that I would never go back to South Beach again. Then the memory of the shame would fade, and new hope would rise. I'll go back, and it'll be different. But it never was.

Now here I am, back at the scene of the crime(s). This time, I am among family. There is no cocaine. There are no drug dealers. Instead there's celebration, tears of joy and victory. Can I handle my first time back? I didn't think I could handle it in 2006, when the Mavericks played the Miami Heat in the championship. Then, I didn't go for fear of what I would become when that plane touched down. I'm amazed by how much you can gradually retrain your mind. That Sunday night in 2008, as I cried and hugged Mark outside the locker room after the Mavericks won, I had no thoughts of drugs and alcohol. I was more than four years into sobriety. I was in honest therapy and retraining my mind. I was focused on the people I was with and our love for each other. "Hey, Brian, we're going to celebrate at a nightclub. We'll see you there!"

Nightclub? Shit! I had not been in a nightclub in years. An environment someone in recovery would obviously try to avoid, not only for the addiction triggers but for the BDD triggers as well. Beautiful people. Lots of comparisons to make. Was I ready? Of course, I didn't want to miss out, but should I skip it for the greater good of Brian? The logical thing would probably have been to not go. My family and Amanda, always supportive of my recovery, made it clear that it was okay with them if I took a pass. I went.

I walked into the club. Drunks everywhere. All kinds of people drinking and having a great time on the dance floor. Dallas Mavericks players up on the stage, rapping and singing. I wanted to enjoy myself, too. I found a seat with Amanda. I drank Diet Cokes. I forced myself to just be a spectator. Then, after I got to hang with my brothers for a while, I simply grew bored. It hit me. The real Brian is a shy guy. In social situations, he is a quiet, sometimes awkward guy. And it's okay. I told that eleven-year-old boy inside me that it's who I was. I can be that person and be happy and productive in my life. I smiled. I kissed Amanda. We danced. I had fun. We left.

June 4, 2012. Testing limits again! Me on television? Holy shit! My own legal segment on a syn-dicated station? Prime territory for my thoughts to start running crazy. However, situations where I per-ceive that I am being judged on what I say instead of how I look are not as stressful for me. I realized this when I had my first appearance on the news in 1999, a time when I was deep in body-dysmorphic thoughts and behaviors. Mark was involved in the possible purchase of the Pittsburgh Penguins hockey team. The owner had declared bankruptcy, and the team was in danger of leaving Pittsburgh. He sent me to Pittsburgh as his "advance man" to evaluate the situation. Naturally, there was a lot of press about him as the hometown guy coming back to save the team. In my role as point person, I got off the plane, and, right there, at the airport gate (pre-9/11, this was allowed), was a television-station crew. My first television interview! As the reporter asked me questions about my brother's interest in the team, I thought to myself: This really is okay. I am not stressed; I can function and speak normally. I used the "one fixed point" theory. The fixed point is not the camera. The fixed point is the person I am speaking with. Of course, watching myself in the in-terview when it aired was different. I couldn't do it. I realized that, while the camera is not a mirror for me, the television, or any type of device that shows me my "reflection" is. Simply put, when the "fixed point" is actually me, that stirs the negative, exaggerated thoughts about myself. My initial reflex is to look away.

In early 2012, I did an interview for a local television station. The subject matter was middle-age drug addicts. In late May of 2012, the same station approached me about being a segment host for a new show called "EyeOpener TV." They wanted me to host a legal segment. While the years of therapy and behavioral mind retraining had certainly taken me to new levels of confidence, I still had self-doubt. Can I hide my love handles on television? Can I hide my receding hairline? Do I need to get another hair transplant? Maybe I can spray-paint my head with that stuff I always see in the magazine on the airplane when I travel. This time, however, my responses are more realistic. Yes, I have love handles. I am over fifty years old. That happens. It's okay. I don't need another hair transplant. What would I get besides more hair? It won't increase my love of myself or the love of others. I have replaced self-loathing and fear with positive thoughts imprinted incrementally during the course of my recovery.

I agreed to do the segment. I may or may not still be doing it when you read this book, but I know I can face the masses and feel good about it regardless of the camera and what anyone on the other side of that camera may be thinking. I still have some negative-projection thoughts, but I evaluate and dismiss them quickly. I have applied this fixed-point coping tactic to interviews, public speaking, and other large-group situations.

Obviously not everyone with BDD will have the opportunity to be in a television series or make media appearances to test their thoughts. But it's important to test them in some way. Start where you think you can handle it. Start as small as you want or as big as you want, but first and foremost, seek out the people who love you. It's normal for us to be afraid of the response. The mind plays strange tricks, even in the face of love. That's why we need support! The ability to love and be loved is the glue that binds together everyone in recovery. Someone wants to help you. Seek them out. Let them help. We are not on this earth to be perfect. We are here to love and be loved.

# EPILOUGE:
## *Walking Toward the Sun*

*A*pril 6, 2013. My father's 87th birthday. My father, of the greatest generation. He fought for his country in the Pacific. He fought in Korea. He took me to my first baseball game more than forty years ago. And he took me in when I was dangerously close to the edge of the abyss.

He's still going strong. And now it's time for us to celebrate his life. How does the Cuban family celebrate? By being together, the way my father stressed that we should live: As a band of brothers. The boys head to Vegas.

Now here I am, decades later, back at that swimming pool. But, now, I'm the old guy. The creaky guy. Not the young fellow who was needlessly embarrassed about taking off his shirt.

I walk through the pool area. The scene hasn't changed. Hard bodies, tattoos, drunks, booze, dancing, and loud music. Déjà-vu. The only thing that has changed is me. I take off my shirt. Nah. Okay, actually,

*Less hair, more fat, it's all good.*

I don't. I'm not showing my fifty-plus-year-old gut in front of these young kids! I think back to my mindset decades before and laugh. So much has changed, but I'm still Brian. I always will be. I rub the top of my balding head. Need to put some sunblock up there! I grab my Diet Coke and take a snooze. Content in my "defects" and not worrying what the crowd might be thinking of me. There will be a nice dinner with the family later. It's all good. As I close my eyes, I can feel the sun. I dream about the next step forward.

❖

CPSIA information can be obtained at www.ICGtesting.com
Printed in the USA
LVOW04s1709190215

427559LV00018B/990/P